HARTLEBURY

Worcestershire

A Record of a Parish

Compiled and Edited by

R.O. Walker

Robert Walker, born and educated in Scotland, pursued a successful career in the Midlands as a consultant dental surgeon specialising in Oral Surgery. His role as a national leader of the profession was recognised by the award of the C.B.E. but much of his professional interests lay in the international field in which he was active in the affairs of the World Health Organisation and the International Dental Federation, travelling widely as a result. Since retiring he has found more time to relax in the countryside of Worcestershire taking an active part in local affairs. The success of his recent publications on the parishes of Shrawley and Witley has encouraged him to believe that this book on Hartlebury will be equally acceptable to those interested in local history.

Published 1987 – Hartlebury Castle Trustees, Hartlebury, Worcestershire DY11 7XX.

Designed and Printed by SPS Print (Birmingham) Ltd

©ISBN-0-9512485-0-2.

Front Cover
East view of Hartlebury Castle by John Smith 1784

Back Cover
Aerial view of Hartlebury Village

CONTENTS

Acknowledgements are due to:

The staff of the Worcestershire County Record Office, The County Museum at Hartlebury Castle and the County Libraries for assistance with research.

The Church Commissioners for details of their Worcestershire Estate.

Wyre Forest and Wychavon District Councils for statistics and details of boundary changes.

Berrows Newspapers, Kidderminster Times and Birmingham Post & Mail for access to archives and permission to reproduce photographs.

The management of Hartlebury Trading Estate, I.M.I. Summerfield, Baggeridge Brick Works and the Central Electricity Generating Board for details of their enterprises.

Glasgow Museum and Art Galleries, Stirling Maxwell Collection for permission to reproduce picture of Pope Clement VII (p.19).

Mrs. Goode for pictures and Legend of Perrins period at Waresley.

Aerofilms for permission to reproduce Aerial View of the village.

Jennifer Grey for providing access to material relative to the State Rooms.

Hilary Brown for preparation of map illustrations.

William Shaw for photography and reproduction of early illustrative material.

Susan Shaw for line drawings in Natural History section.

Mary Parsons for proof reading.

Mrs. Alison Gibbons for access to records of the Gibbons family and of her father Mr. H. Eliot Howard.

Mr. Tony Bishop for his account of No. 25 Maintenance Unit of the R.A.F.

Mr. Reg Abbott for information on the Hartlebury gipsies.

Mrs. Lynne Parsons for research into the inns of Hartlebury.

Mr. Michael Oliver for permission to photograph "West Tip".

and to those countless individuals who have provided information, anecdotes and material for illustrations.

The Editor would also wish to apologise to others who had indicated a willingness to be interviewed. Unfortunate circumstances prevented him from following these up and thus some parts of the story may be incomplete. Hopefully there are no inaccuracies.

INTRODUCTION

The recent upsurge of interest in local history among the general public would be sufficient justification in itself for the publication of a book on the Parish of Hartlebury. The presence, however, within its bounds for many centuries of Hartlebury Castle, the historic See House of the Diocese of Worcester, adds a unique dimension and provides much of the material upon which its past history is based.

Following an introductory account of present day topography and natural history and a brief dip into some facets of early history, the major part of the first half of this work will, therefore, be devoted to the architectural history of the Castle, with an account of some of its distinguished occupants. A series of essays which follow will reflect life in the building in the nineteenth and twentieth centuries, based upon a recently discovered diary and the recollections of individuals, culminating in an account of the historic events of 1956-64 which led to important changes in its use.

History becomes very much alive in individuals' recollection of events which have occurred within living memory and many have been generous in sharing these with the editor, so adding colour to the concluding section on "The Changing Face of Hartlebury" in which the story of life in the parish during this century is portrayed. Time, however, has not permitted of anything but a superficial search through the local archives, a rewarding task which must be left to others, stimulated perhaps by the introduction which this publication offers. The B.B.C. Domesday survey of 1985 with its access to computerised technology, will certainly open a new chapter in facilitating the recording and interpretation of future knowledge and doubtless accelerate the momentum of interest in what can be a most rewarding and fascinating field of study.

I am grateful to Bishop Philip Goodrich for the invitation to compile this history and to Mrs. Charles-Edwards and Bishop Robin Woods for assistance in drafting the section on the period 1956-81.

Others have been generous in the gift of their time and talents and to them must be addressed any comment or criticism of their contributions. For the remainder of the text the Editor accepts responsibility in the hope that he has accurately reflected the facts or opinions expressed.

Acknowledgements will recognise other sources of information and illustrations. No specific references are included directly in the text, but an extensive bibliography gives an indication of the major works consulted and many individuals, too numerous to mention, have welcomed me into their homes and provided me with the pleasure of making new acquaintances and some abiding friendships. None more so, however, than Miss Molly Symonds and Mr. Edgar Sobey, who acted as my guides through the tortuous paths of discovering a new parish.

In this day of computers, it must be unusual for an Editor to rely upon his own longhand script, scissors and sellotape with which to process words into a form suitable for publication. Judith Dickinson has been more than generous and patient in typing and retyping the entire manuscript, and to her and to John Mills, who has once again provided the advice on presentation, printing and publication, I am more than grateful. A few of the illustrations are taken from old and somewhat faded photographs with resulting loss of definition but are justified because of their especial interest.

R.O. Walker,
The Knapp
Shrawley,
Worcester.

FOREWORD

If you live in Hartlebury or have known it in the past, this series of essays is a must. There is something about history, the story of its roads, the description of its flora and fauna, delightful pictures of life not only in a medieval bishop's castle, but also in a nineteenth century home. Did you know that Hartlebury once had ten pubs; that the Mitre Oak was on the main road from Holyhead to London; that once there was a large deer park round the Castle which had an impressive gatehouse and tower? Those who are interested in the story of a great historic house will read the essays eagerly. There is also plenty about Hartlebury today with its trading estate and its new look.

On any showing, Hartlebury is a village of great interest. From times before the Conquest there must have been many comings and goings. Bishop Giffard had a retinue of 140 riders. Later in the Middle Ages as many as 100 soldiers were stationed in the Castle. Within living memory the Bishop had a butler, three housemaids, three kitchen maids, three gardeners and a chauffeur, and but the day before yesterday, the Queen had lunch there and the Prince of Wales stayed with Bishop Robin Woods who had been at one time the equivalent of the Royal Family's parish priest.

I am more grateful than I can say to Dr. Walker for having undertaken the heavy task of compiling and editing this book. I want everyone in the village and beyond to have the opportunity of reading it. Those who want to study the story and indeed the future shape of villages will want to read these essays and at the back there is an excellent list of books for those who want to take their researches further.

That there is a Bishop still living in Hartlebury is remarkable. It can only be because two-thirds of the Castle have been put to other use. The north wing, as everyone knows, is the County Museum, and in the middle are the State Rooms which are run by Trustees who need the financial support which is necessary if these lovely rooms are to be kept for many people to enjoy. I cannot therefore disguise the fact that we hope this book will be a best-seller and bring in funds for the upkeep of the State Rooms.

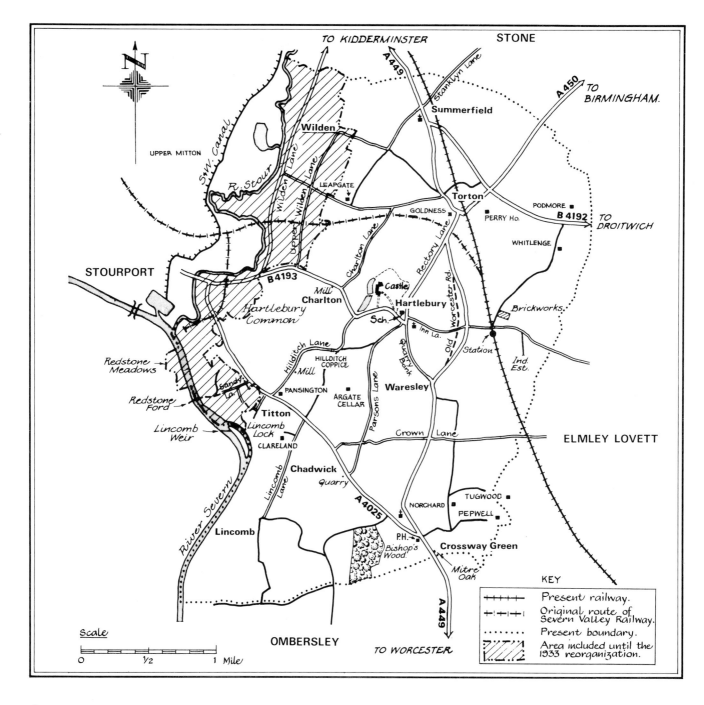

TOPOGRAPHY

The Parish of Hartlebury, one of the larger in the County of Hereford and Worcester, is situated in the District of Wychavon; quadrilateral in shape, it is bounded to the north by the parishes of Stone and Wilden - the latter now a ward of Stourport - to the east by Elmley Lovett, to the south by Ombersley and to the west by Stourport. The Severn from Lincomb Lock to Hampstall Ferry is also part of the western boundary.

The boundary of the Manor of Hartlebury in 1648 is described in detail in a Parliamentary Survey.

"From the Mitre Oak to a village called Wynnald in the Parish of Ombersley; go westwards to the River Severn to Redstone Ferry, including the ferry and Redstone Meadow (on the west bank). At the end of the meadow come back again including half of the Severn up till Stourmouth; there go up the Stour till Wilden Mills and on to Lower Morses and a field called Lowe Field and most part of the heath up to a little mound on the heath dividing this Manor from Stone; so including Tortonfield to a place called Bounds and then to a place called Hargreaves and so to a place called Hagg Lane - on to Pye Hill and along Walton Field to Pepwell Farm and back to Mitre Oak."

Originally covering some 5714 acres, two major changes since the middle of the nineteenth century have served to reduce this to its present size of 4552 acres. First, the advent of the Staffordshire and Worcestershire Canal in 1771 to the hamlet of Mitton, which resulted in its development as Stourport, prior to which it was but a community of a few houses with a small inn, the "Stour Mouth", thought to be by the site of today's "Old Anchor". The "district" of Stourport then formed, consisted of Lower Mitton, by then a part of the Parish of Kidderminster, and Upper Mitton in the Parish of Hartlebury. When these two were formally united as the Parish of Stourport in 1844, Upper Mitton with its 359 acres was ceded.

The second boundary revision took place in 1933 when, as the result of a Local Government Act of that year, that part of Hartlebury Common known as Lower Heath, together with a few meadows previously held on the west bank of the Severn beside the Redstone Ferry, were transferred to Stourport Urban District at the same time as Wilden became independent resulting in the loss of a further 803 acres.

The centre of the Parish is the village which lies two miles from Stourport, six from Droitwich, four from Kidderminster, eleven from Worcester and twenty-five from Birmingham, with good communicating roads. Three main highways traverse the parish: the A449 from Worcester, now a new dual carriageway started in 1936 and completed in stages by 1978, which bypasses the main centres of population and which enters at Crossway Green, continues past Waresley, before proceeding to Kidderminster: the A4025 which leaves the A449 at Crossway Green and passes through Chadwick and Titton across the Common and on to Stourport, and the B4193 which runs from Stourport to Charlton, past Hartlebury Castle and through the village proper before joining the A449 via Rectory Lane. From the B4193 run two important lanes, Quarry Bank, which leaves the village and continues up Waresley Road to join the A449 at Waresley; and Inn Lane, which leaves Rectory Lane to join the Old Worcester Road by the Talbot Inn.

Many other narrow lanes serve to join the several hamlets, the more important being Parsons Lane from the village to Chadwick, Hillditch Lane from Charlton to Titton, Crown Lane from Chadwick across the A449 to Elmley Lovett, Lincomb Lane from Titton to Lincomb and Charlton Lane which runs from Charlton to join the A449 at Torton. The profusion of other narrow Devonshire-type lanes which extend southward from the Common into the neighbouring Parish of Ombersley, is some indication of an early establishment of hamlets and smallholdings in this especially fertile part of the Severn Valley.

The Great Western Railway line from the South-West to the North Midlands, opened in 1852, greatly improved communications with the outside world, but it was in 1862 when the Severn Valley Railway was opened as a branch line from Hartlebury via Stourport and Bewdley to Shrewsbury that the Hartlebury Junction became an even more important link in the transport services of the district. In addition to its passenger services, it provided a more speedy outlet for products of local industry and in particular for perishable farm produce. Sadly the branch line closed in 1963 - although it has lately been redeveloped as a tourist attraction between Kidderminster and Bridgnorth. The station is now an unmanned "HALT" with no stationmaster and a very limited passenger service.

The loss of Upper Mitton in 1844 and the boundary adjustments of 1933 which also involved the loss of considerable population, make comparisons of growth in recent years difficult, especially since no census returns are available for 1941, but with a population today of 2402 (1981 census) compared with 2514 in 1911, a significant figure is that the number of households in the reduced area has increased by 189 between 1951 and 1981.

Prior to the Second World War, Hartlebury was a parish recognised mainly by the presence of a castle, the See House of the Diocese of Worcester, with its history dating back to the seventh century and a large area of "common" used as a public recreational area and a site of special interest to naturalists. This self-sufficient rural community, content to enjoy the patronage of the incumbent of the Castle and to get on with the task of tilling the land and reaping a harvest, was to be transformed by the arrival in 1938 of a Royal Air Force Maintenance Unit to the east of the railway line and in 1940 of a small arms factory at Summerfield. Until then a small but successful brickworks established in 1885, was the only sign of heavy industry. Both of these more recent enterprises remain today, but with their purposes changed: the former now developed as a Trading Estate and the latter as an Ordnance Unit responsible for the design, development and production of rocket motors.

The Castle also has recently been the subject of significant change. As a home for bishops it was now much too large and following prolonged negotiations between the Diocese and the Church Commissioners, a remodelling programme was completed in 1964 which provided not only more suitable modern living accommodation for the Bishop, but made arrangements for the State Rooms to become a centre for social and cultural activities as well as providing space for a County Museum whose objective is "to illustrate the broad basis of the life of the Worcestershire people through the centuries".

Until 1939 the everyday needs of the people had been largely catered for by local traders and agriculture provided the bulk of employment, but all this was to change. Farming became mechanised, nearby towns competed with shop-keepers and trades-men for the custom of a public now free to move with the increased availability of motorised transport. An awakening of interest on the part of urban dwellers, to the attractions of the countryside, combined with the release of accommodation previously required for farm workers and the relaxation of restrictions on new building, transformed the village, like so many others, into an attractive dor-mitory for a commuting public. Three general stores, two Post Offices, two garages and five public houses survive, but these only by changing with the times to satisfy the much more demanding needs of a new generation.

All rural parishes, however, and Hartlebury is no exception, still depend heavily upon a successful farming community. The Triassic Sandstone belt upon which the greater part of the parish lies, provides a light easily worked soil suitable for mixed arable farming. It also provides favourable conditions for market garden-ing, enhanced by the relative immunity from frosts. The dramatic changes which have taken place in agricultural methods will be referred to later (p.51).

Hartlebury Common today occupies about 216 acres of the parish but this is much less than previously when before enclosure and reclamation of a substantial part for agricultural purposes, it extended northwards and to the east of the River Stour as far as Hoobrook and Torton, bordering on today's Kidderminster. The present area of open heathland lies on two separate levels separated by an escarpment. The upper is covered extensively by gorse and broom with some oak woodland, bracken and heather, while the lower terrace which includes some woodland and scrub is basically a rich dry heathland. The "Social and Natural History of Hartlebury Common" has recently been the subject of a research project spon-sored and published by the Hereford and Worcester County Council. Its findings suggest that the heathy nature of the

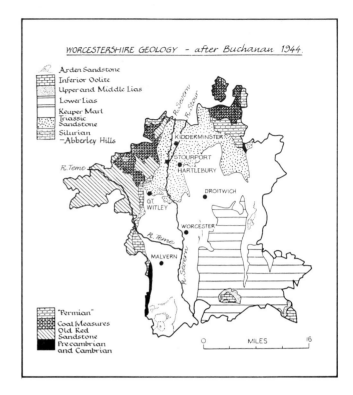

Common is probably of Iron Age origin as the result of woodland clearance, subsequent over-grazing and over-cropping. The Enclosure Act of 1815 in favour of Hartlebury Parish, and a subsequent award of 1821 saw that the top two-thirds of "Hartle-bury Heath" was enclosed and thus the present extent protected. Commoners rights for grazing no longer apply but a handful of individuals are still able to claim free access to sand. Its main purpose is now well established as a site of Special Scientific Interest (1956) and a Local Nature Reserve (1979) with strict rules for its use as a recreational area - much enjoyed by the public - clearly laid down by the County Council as owners of the land.

In company with the rapid changes which have taken place in the economic and social structure of the nation during this century and especially since the Second World War, life in rural communities has changed beyond recognition and the role of the church, schools and local tradesmen has been revolutionised. "The Changing Face of Hartlebury" will therefore be the title of a later chapter in which the reflections and recollections of parishioners will provide the background to a fascinating and for some nostalgic story. Newcomers to the district may also learn something of the more recent history of this attractive part of Worcestershire.

NATURAL HISTORY.

by J.J. Day

The western boundary of the parish is marked by two main features, the River Severn and Hartlebury Common. The lowest point, some seventeen metres, is on the flood plain on the Severn, and the highest point, approximately one hundred and eight metres, is near Bishop's Wood. The greater part is situated on an undulating plateau, over forty metres high, which is dissected by various small stream valleys, the most important of which is Titton Brook. Most of the parish drains into this brook and thus into the River Severn just north of Lincomb Lock, while the remaining small portion to the east drains into the Hadley Brook.

Geologically most of the area (about 80%) is on the Lower Keuper Sandstone. In the south-east of the parish (about 10% of the area) there is an outcrop of Keuper Marl which produces heavy, poorly drained clays. The final 10% overlies a variety of geological formations including Lower Mottled Sandstone, Blown Sand, Gravel River Terraces in the north-west and alluvial soils in the stream and river valleys. The clay which now provides the raw material for a modern brickworks doubtless at one time also provided the material for crucibles which were used in local forges, while the softer sand from the Common was suitable for making moulds. The harder outcrops of Red Sandstone were a ready local source of building material, especially foundations for timber-framed houses.

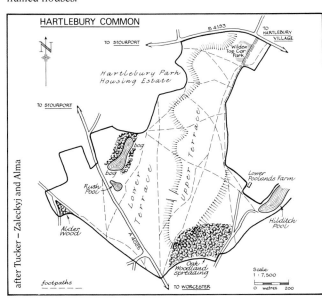

Most of the parish is given over to intensive arable farming. Less than 11% produces good wildlife habitat, and of this nearly a half is on Hartlebury Common, one of the finest wildlife habitats in the county, the remainder being associated with the river and stream valleys, particularly the River Severn and Titton Brook, where cultivation is difficult due to steep slopes or retarded drainage, the one major exception to this rule being Bishop's Wood near Crossway Green.

Hartlebury Common

Woodlands There are thirty-two woods occupying about sixty-one hectares*, mostly supporting native broad-leaved species. Sixty-two per cent of this is ecologically valuable ancient semi-natural woodland, distributed amongst nine sites. Most of the remainder is either recent plantations or secondary invasions of oak and birch on open valley sides or common land and these are much less valuable for wildlife. The largest and richest woods are Bishop's Wood, Hillditch Coppice, Lincomb River Cliff and Lincomb Bank, all others being less than two hectares.

Bishop's Wood is a fine example of an oak/birch woodland. It holds both species of native oaks, holly, aspen, rowan and hazel and a ground flora dominated by acid-loving species such as foxglove, hard fern, bracken, soft grass, wood sorrel; it also has a very rich fungi flora. The greatest loss to the parish's wildlife resource in recent years has been associated with the clear felling of a considerable part of this ancient woodland in the course of the construction of the Central Electricity Generating Board Plant, and very recently the clearance for agricultural purposes of most of the eastern sector, a total irreparable loss of thirty per cent of the parish's already sparse and valuable woodland.

The Lincomb River Cliff and Bank holds a wet willow/alder wood at the northern end but most of the site is on the steep valleyside which supports oak and lime. Such woods are rare in the county and this is a good representative example of its type.

* one hectare = 2.47 acres.

3

Hillditch Coppice holds two distinct woodland types. The valley is occupied by alder carr whereas the steep slopes of the valley are unusual and in part derive from nineteenth century plantings, including fine beech, hornbeam and sweet chestnut trees. The ground flora is rich and includes the rare thin-spiked wood sedge. This is one of only three Worcestershire sites for the fly honeysuckle. In most years the wood attracts numbers of wintering chaffinches and bramblings with the occasional hawfinch.

A notable feature of the parish's woods are seven alder woodlands, a rare type in the county. Alder supports a rich association of plants and animals, including birds such as the spotted woodpecker, siskin and redpoll. The redpoll is a small finch which feeds on birch and alder seed, and within the last twenty years has colonised Worcestershire and now breeds in the parish. The flora includes many wetland species such as marsh marigold, yellow iris, hemp agrimony, valerian and greater bitter cress. The latter species is almost totally confined to such woods in North Worcestershire.

In addition to the woodlands proper, there are about fifteen hectares of old parkland and large well-wooded gardens, which increase the woodland resource. The best area adjoins the Castle. This has a fine stand of lime trees and a variety of old parkland trees.

Scrub and Grassland About seven hectares of scrub and species rich grassland is found mainly on steep slopes. The areas of scrub are mainly thorn and gorse. One field supports a very rich flora, including an abundance of the rare meadow saxifrage, Saxifraga Granulata. The remaining grasslands of interest are acid types.

Marshland is a rapidly decreasing habitat throughout Britain and is one of Worcestershire's rarest habitats. Hartlebury has about eight hectares of marsh, all lying on alluvial soils in riparian situations. Marshland has a very distinctive flora and the Hartlebury sites are fairly rich, supporting species such as ragged robin, devil's bit scabious, marsh marigold, marsh and spotted orchids. Breeding birds include reed bunting, sedge warbler and yellow wagtail and formerly redshank and snipe.

In addition to these nutrient rich fens, there is a small acid bog on the Common. This is Worcestershire's only example of this type of habitat. It has a rich flora including plants such as the insectivorous sundew, cranberry, in their only county localities and some others such as cross-leaved heath, cotton grass and bog pondweed which are rare elsewhere.

Open Water The western boundary of the parish is marked by the River Severn. This large river, being navigated, has little aquatic vegetation and is poor in breeding birds. The banks, however, are tree-lined and provide a well-wooded wildlife corridor. The river itself, generally regarded as clean, supports a good fish population and a moderately rich invertebrate fauna, including the nationally rare club-tailed dragonfly and the scarce white-legged damselfly. Unfortunately, industrial pollution from the River Stour is still a problem downstream from Stourport, but some recovery in quality does occur before reaching Worcester.

Lamprey and Lampern were at one time common in the Severn and Campden's recipe (1695) for their dressing is interesting: "Kill them in Malmsey (a strong sweet wine), stop their mouths with nutmegs and their holes with cloves and roll them round with pounded filberts (hazelnuts), crumbs of bread, oil, malmsey and spices and stew in a pan for a few minutes". Doubtless a real delicacy.

Most of the eleven kilometres of other watercourses are rather small and of limited wildlife value, apart from providing wildlife corridors. The Titton Brook is a medium-sized, fast-flowing stream with a sandy and gravelly bed and moderately rich invertebrate fauna. The birds, dippers and grey wagtails, are occasionally seen.

Between thirty and forty small ponds occupy about two hectares. Most are associated with stream valleys, farms or woods. This is a very low density for the county as a whole and is a reflection of the freely drained soils and the preponderance of arable land. Many of these ponds have a very limited wildlife value, being in a derelict condition.

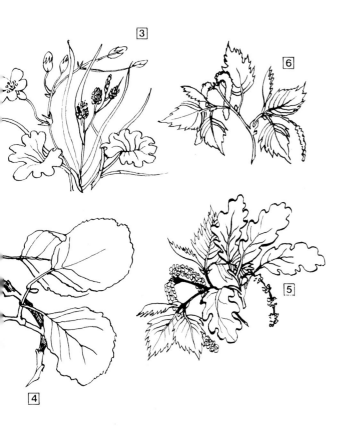

Nine larger pools occupy about six hectares. The most valuable for wildlife are Hillditch Pool*, with its well-developed reedswamp community; Hartlebury Castle Pools with their water-lilies and breeding tufted duck and Rush Pool on Hartlebury Common with its very interesting flora which includes several rare species, marsh cinquefoil, floating club-rush, bogbean and pale sedge.

Heathland Hartlebury Common is one of the finest examples of a lowland, dwarf-shrub heath in the West Midlands and is now managed as a Local Nature Reserve by the Hereford and Worcester County Council. It is mainly sited on blown sand and old river terraces (gravels), and exhibits some of the best examples of inland blown dunes in Britain. The area of heath occupies about eighty-seven hectares (4.7% of the parish) and can be divided floristically into six main zones. Two of these, the acid bog and the woodlands, are mentioned elsewhere.

The land west of the A4025, the Lower Terrace, supports a rich and dense flora, a mixture of heather heath, scrub and grassland. The middle part of the common is principally dominated by heather with frequent open sandy areas, while the eastern Upper Terrace holds a tract of dry dwarf shrub heath with ling, bell heather, broom, western gorse and bracken. Dividing the Upper and Middle Terraces is a very steep slope. This zone shows the best examples of bare dunes.

The heathland flora is rich, particularly in the species associated with the open sandy areas. Some of the plants are not found anywhere else in the county, for example striated catchfly, or have only a few other stations, e.g. shepherd's cress, viper's bugloss, heath rush, flixweed, buckshorn plantain, slender cudweed, spring vetch, fieldmouse ear, hoary cinquefoil. The heath also supports a wide variety of invertebrates including a number of rare moths and spiders, as well as a healthy population of lizards, a species now much declined in the county. Of birds, several heathland specialists such as nightjar, red-backed shrike, woodlark and stonechat were once plentiful but have now disappeared. However, meadow and tree pipits as well as redpoll, cuckoo and many commoner species still breed.

Hartlebury Common is a unique habitat in the West Midlands and hopefully its future is now assured.

Other habitats Due to intensive cultivation and the lack of stock rearing, the parish as a whole has a much lower density of hedges than other parts of the county. Many of those that remain are low in

1. Yellow Wagtail, Willow Sedge and Bittercress   2. Saxifrage   3. Saxifrage and Pale Sedge   4. Alder   5. Birch and Oak   6. Birch   7. Oak   8. Wood Sorrel and Bracken

* It has only recently been announced that the World Wildlife Fund has made a grant to Hereford and Worcester County Council for the purchase of the nine acre site which includes Hillditch Pool and Coppice, which is rich in flowers such as pink water speedwell, great hairy willow herb, skull cap, wild angelica and lady's smock. The site will now be conserved and managed by the Countryside Service of the County Council.

species, gappy and in general have a very limited wildlife value. Only the roadside hedgebanks provide any interesting flora. The cultivated land has its own specialised weed flora different from the heavy clay soils which occupy most of the county. Plants such as field bugloss, least bird's foot, corn marigold, storksbill, red spurrey occur as arable weeds in the parish but are rare away from the area. Most of the orchards are intensively managed and have a low wildlife potential.

Two railway lines cross the parish; the working Kidderminster-Droitwich line and the now disused branch line to Stourport. The disused line is beginning to develop into an interesting site with tree and scrub invasion plus areas of more open habitats and acid grassland. The small toadflax has been found here. The working line supports areas of rough grassland and scrub of moderate wildlife interest. In total, the railways now represent a significant part of the parish's wildlife habitat

Conservation The parish has about one hundred and ninety-six hectares of reasonable wildlife habitat not including hedgerows, road verges or orchards. Much of this is concentrated on the Common, which is the most outstanding wildlife feature and is now a Nature Reserve. The second most important site, Bishop's Wood, has suffered irreparable damage recently but part of it is now managed as an educational nature reserve by the Central Electricity Generating Board. No other sites have formal protection. If the wildlife resource of the parish is to be retained, the other valuable habitats mentioned above must be spared from further degradation by sympathetic management and the badgers allowed to continue to play at Titton and nearby Winnal.

H. ELIOT HOWARD.

No account of the wildlife of Hartlebury would be complete without reference to the distinguished ornithologist, H. Eliot Howard. Clareland in Titton, a lovely nineteenth century, two storey brick-built house, was his home for forty years from 1900 - 1940 and he managed to combine a successful career as an industrialist with a lifetime's interest in wildlife, particularly birds. Most of his work was done in the early hours of the morning on Hartlebury Common and at Lincomb Lock before setting off on his bicycle for Kidderminster Station. He was ably supported by his wife, an ardent botanist, who kept copious notes and wrote up much of her husband's work.

He has been described as a shy and friendly person who avoided public meetings and enjoyed the company of a few close friends. He was a scholar - he read Plato at breakfast - and a philosopher, methodical and infinitely painstaking in his methods. His records earned him an international reputation, but he declined invitations to broadcast or lecture abroad. His main interest was bird behaviour to which end he would take one or more pairs of

H. Eliot Howard with record salmon

birds each year and follow their habits in great detail, travelling further afield if this should be necessary. His main published works, copies of which are the proud possessions of his family and a few close friends, were:-

> **British Warblers** - which came out in nine parts between 1907 and 1914 and was finally bound in two volumes. This beautiful publication was illustrated by a Dane, Henrik Gronvold.
> **Territory in Bird Life** - 1920 - is still today the authoritative work and has been extended to apply to the entire animal kingdom.
> **An Introduction to the Study of Bird Behaviour** - 1929.
> **The Nature of a Bird's World** - 1929.
> **The Water Hen's World** based upon the pool in the garden at Clareland - 1939.

These last four books were illustrated by George Lodge. Many other contributions appeared in the proceedings of various Natural History and other scientific societies.

It is nice to know that he could also relax fishing below the weir at Lincomb and that the cock salmon caught there on a spinning minnow and weighing 43 lbs, measuring 48 3/4 inches in length and with a girth of 25 inches, is still a record for the Severn.

EARLY HISTORY

The spelling of Hartlebury has changed many times over the centuries being originally derived from HEORTLA - a diminutive for HEOROT - meaning HART and BYRIG - an enclosed or fortified place, thus Heortlabyrig in 817, Huerteberie in 1086, Hertlebur in the thirteenth century and Hurtbery in the sixteenth century.

The area must have provided attractions for early settlers with its good communications by track or river, a fertile soil and ample other natural resources but almost certainly, the determining factor for the establishment of a settlement was the proximity of two of the easier crossings of the River Severn at Redstone and Larford Fords. A letter from Bishop Latimer to Lord Cromwell stated "hereby is a hermitage in a rock by the Severn able to lodge 500 men", and according to Habingdon "there appears on the very front of the hermitage the arms of England between those of Beauchamp, Earl of Warwick and those of Mortimer". The hermitage was later converted into dwellings and then into a school. Nearby rocky prominences also provided good defensive positions. Evidence that the site was used by the Romans is available in the discovery at Lincomb of a bronze coin of the Emperor Alexander period. The Roman occupation had reached the level of the Severn and Trent by AD47 and lasted till the early fifth century when it was followed by a sequence of disturbing invasions into the area by Anglo-Saxons and Danes, not forgetting the occasional forays into Worcestershire of the Welsh.

Christianity came to the Severn Valley in the seventh century at a time when Gloucestershire and Worcestershire and a large part of South Warwickshire were occupied by the HWICCE, a pagan group, vassals of the more powerful Mercians to the north, and in 680 the Worcester Diocese began its somewhat precarious existence as the Diocese of Hwicce. In the ninth century the Anglo-Saxon Kingdom of Mercia extended from the North Sea to the Severn and was ruled by Burthred who, as was customary in those days, looked to the Church for effective military support. Recognising, like others before him, the strategic importance of the Hartlebury site, he acquired the Manor and awarded it to the then Bishop, AELHUN, in 860.

The Manor of Hartlebury at that time, with its area of over 4000 acres, was virtually identical with the Parish except for the existence of the small adjoining holding of MITUNE (Mitton). The separation of Waresley to become another manor came in 980 when five manses were leased by Bishop Oswald to his clerk Wulgar. That marvellous historical compendium - the Domesday Book - originally designed to locate national resources for the purposes of tax and defence, provides confirmation of the situation in 1086.

"The same Church holds HUERTEBERIE with six berewicks. There, are twenty hides, and in demesne four ploughs, twenty-four villeins, three bordars, and a Priest,

River Severn in the early days *(by kind permission of Bewdley Museum)*

having twenty-one ploughs among them all. There, are twelve serfs three serving women, two mills of four shillings, and ten seams of corn. Wood a mile long and half a mile wide, and five houses in Wich rending five mitts of salt. In the time of King Edward it was worth sixteen pounds; its present value is thirteen pounds and ten shillings."

METTUNE (Mitton) is mentioned briefly as one of sixteen berwicks in the King's holding of the Manor of Kidderminster which "was all waste" and again as MITUNE under the Bishop of Hereford's holding of the Manor of Bredon as "one hide appropriate to the sustenance of monks".

Confirmation of this early existence of Mitton in two parts appears in 1221 and 1420 when we find the first references to Over (Upper) and Nether (Lower) Mitton respectively.

Pearce writing in his History of Hartlebury Castle states that it is "perhaps safe to guess" that of the six berwicks attributed to Hartlebury, one was Waresley, another Upper Mitton, a third at Whytlench and a fourth Pepwell "but the evidence of the earlier separate existence of Mitton and Waresley is strong and of the other claimants to recognition we have no knowledge".

The population of Hartlebury in those early days, given as 187, must be placed in the perspective of the total county population of 4724 and a national estimate of two million. In the same context the bishop and the cathedral in 1086 held one third of the total acreage of the county and Worcester was ranked as the fourth richest prelacy in the country. The great bulk of the parish was thus owned by the bishop and remained so until 1553 following which it passed through various hands until the Restoration in 1660.

The Black Death came to England in 1348. Bishop Bransford remained secluded in his Manor, but in spite of these precautions, died on the 6th August 1349 and the condition of the estate at that time was accounted as follows:

"Tenants could not be got at any price, mills were vacant, forges standing idle, pigeon houses in ruins with all the

Berewick - a hamlet within a larger Manor.
Hide - approximately 120 acres.
Plough - as much land as can be ploughed by a yoke of oxen in one day, later limited by statute to one acre.
Demesne - land normally retained for the protection and sole use of the lord.
Villeins - serfs who enjoyed tenancy at the lord's pleasure.
Bordars - villeins of a low order - holders of a cottage and plot of land in return for a service.
Manse - a measure of land regarded as sufficient for the support of a family - in effect taken to approximate to a hide.

Most entries in Domesday refer to a specified acreage of woodland and the reference to salt indicates the importance placed on those commodities. Wood from Hartlebury was used for the salt boilings at Droitwich. The small population figures in Domesday must be interpreted in the light of the total population of the county at that time - 4724.

birds fled. Half the cash owing to the Bishop was never paid on account of the death of tenants who were wont to pay rent and of customary tenants who all died in the deadly pestilence."

As late as 1354 relief was still being sought on the grounds that it was impossible for the Bishop to obtain any of the customary services. Forty-five per cent of all parish priests died and probably one third of the populace. Many holdings were left without tenants and these were available for distribution among the remainder, providing larger and more viable plots for the fortunate few.

The plague revisited the parish in 1604/5 when ten people died between October and January.

Further changes, however, were soon to come, for with the declining influence of the Manorial system under the Tudors, the parish assumed greater administrative responsibility and, while remaining answerable to the established Church, actual ownership of the land began to pass to a new aristocracy. By 1860 that part of the parish still retained by the Church had come under the jurisdiction of the Ecclesiastical Commissioners, now the Church Commissioners, who still own the Manorial rights. The holding today, however, is much reduced to just over 427 acres, 417 of which comprise two farms completely surrounding the Castle. The balance of ten acres comprises the Castle buildings, its immediate grounds together with the pool and moat and that part leased to the County Council for the purposes of the County Museum. The Hartlebury land today is one of two blocks - the other is at Grimley - which together make up the Worcester Estate inherited from the Bishopric of Worcester in 1948. Tenant farmers are still occasionally invited to dine in the Great Hall - the Bishop presiding.

With the Severn for so many centuries navigable as far up as Shrewsbury, with one of the better fording places at Redstone and with the Bishop of Worcester securely established at the Castle, which was fortified in the thirteenth century, it is not surprising that Hartlebury as a rural community prospered and that small service industries grew up. Bishop Giffard (1268-1302) leased a corn mill at Charlton to Adam de Hartlebery and Agnes his wife. Fulling and dyeing mills were established beside the River Stour (1299), and although dates are not available it seems likely that the corn mill and tannery at Titton, the spinning mill at Jenny Hole and the forges, notably at Wilden, were soon to follow. It is recorded that scythes, a basic agricultural requirement, were made in 1564 and that in 1841 as many as 398 smiths were engaged here and in adjoining parishes.

Interesting as the early history may be there can be no doubt however that the presence of a See house for the Diocese of Worcester within the parish for over a thousand years has been a dominant influence and it is to the story of this period that we now turn.

HARTLEBURY CASTLE

THE ARCHITECTURAL HISTORY.

by N.A.D. Molyneux

The Castle stands in the midst of parkland, which was once filled with deer. It is today approached along a seventeenth century lime avenue, originally planted by Bishop Edward Stillingfleet (1689-99) and stands on a plateau of red sandstone with a moat on three sides. The moat to the west is still filled with water, and is the remnant of an extensive medieval system of fish ponds which once filled the two valleys isolating the plateau.

The Bishop of Worcester was given land in Hartlebury by the King of Mercia in the 860s AD, but the earliest mention of an episcopal house is in 1268 when Godfrey Giffard succeeded Walter Cantilupe as Bishop. Henry III granted Giffard the right to crenellate an existing building which Cantilupe had begun to fortify with a moat and stone wall. Crenellation (adding battlements to the walls) was as much a piece of social cachet as an actual defensive measure.

This was by no means the Bishop's only residence in the Diocese. He divided his stays between the various episcopal manors notably at Alvechurch, where he kept his herd of deer, Bibury, Blockley, Bredon, Hampton-on-Avon, Hartlebury, Henbury -in-the-Saltmarsh, Kempsey, Wick, Withington, and the Palace in Worcester. Over the centuries successive bishops concentrated their stays at Alvechurch, Hartlebury and Worcester until, in the seventeenth century, Alvechurch went out of use and was demolished; the Palace at Worcester still stands, with substantial vaulted undercrofts from Giffard's time. At Hartlebury there are no traces of Giffard's building save for the moat which he completed.

The Medieval Fabric of the Castle is now ascribed to Bishop Henry Wakefield (1375-95) having been previously assigned to the later period of Bishop John Carpenter (1444-76). The most obvious feature today is the Great Hall which retains a medieval roof and walls. The wall posts of the six roof trusses rise from stone corbels and are jointed to the principal rafters forming jointed crucks. The collars are supported by arch braces with two raking struts above which vanish into the plaster ceiling inserted later. There is no evidence for a fourteenth century chimney stack, a hearth in the middle of the floor probably serving for heating, the smoke escaping through a louvre on the roof.

Within a tall bay (or oriel) window, situated where the present porch is, stood the bishop's throne, placed on a raised dais with the lower ranks accommodated below. The entrance to the Hall would be via a screens passage at the north from an outer door which was removed when this end was later rebuilt. This same area contained the buttery, pantry and servants' quarters with the kitchen as a nearby detached building, normal practice in large houses in those days. Evidence of two original windows, visible

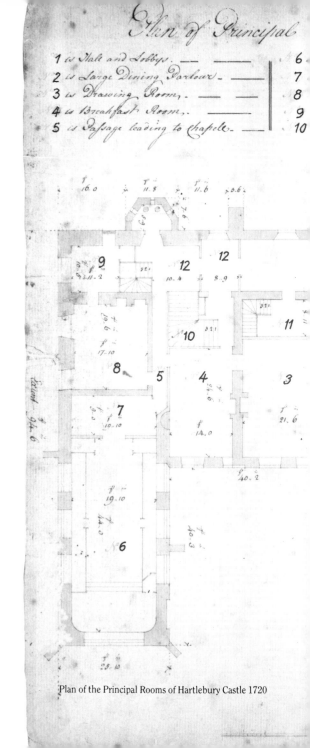

Plan of the Principal Rooms of Hartlebury Castle 1720

11 is Butlers Pantry.

12 are Lobbys

13 is Long Passage.

14 is Smoaking Room.

15 is Stewards Room.

16 is Kitchen

17 is Scullary to Do.

18 is Larder to Kitchen,

19 is Staircase

20 is Servants Hall.

21 is Houskeepers Room,

22 is Laundry

23 is Washhouse

24 is Granery.

25 is Brewhouse.

26 is Dairy

27 is Scullary to Do.

28 is Room to Do.

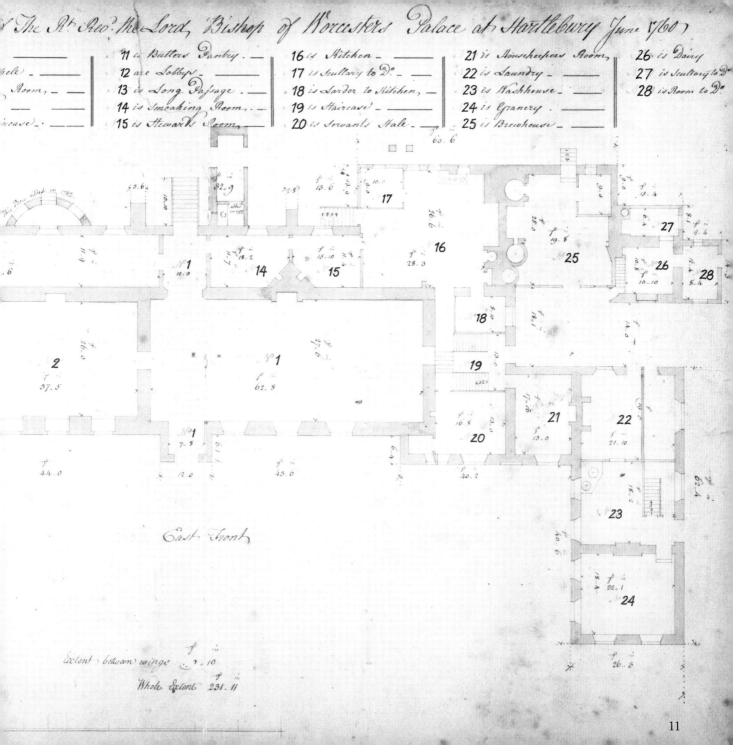

East Front

Extent between wings   .10

Whole Extent 231.11

11

from the outside, remains high up on the west wall, each with two cinquefoil lights under a square head.

The south end contained the bishop's private rooms with the new chamber (nova camera) in which Bishop Wakefield is known to have received one Reginald Henbury, in 1386. This was in or near the present bishop's study. Only the walls of the chapel date from the fourteenth century but details of the original are recorded. Habington, writing in the seventeenth century, gives a detailed description of the heraldry of the original glazing which enables it to be dated within the last two decades of the fourteenth century. Buck's print of the castle in 1731 shows the east window with its interesting tracery. The roof of this wing was then low pitched, covered with lead, unlike the rest of the roofs of the building which were tile clad.

In 1395/6, twenty great oaks were brought to Hartlebury Castle from the Manor of Welland, presumably to build the roof of the Hall as we see it today, an indication that Wakefield, who died in 1395, did not however see the completion of the building.

Bishop Carpenter did, however, make his mark on the Castle. Leland, writing in the 1540s, tells us that Carpenter built a gate house, and this is confirmed by the recorded expenditure on his houses at Hartlebury and Worcester in 1460/1, 1467/8 and 1469/70. These dates correspond with his periods of residence. He was absent in 1460/62, whilst works were in progress, spending most of his time at Alvechurch, but he was more or less continually at Hartlebury from 1471/73, just after work was completed. In building a gatehouse, he was following the fashion of the time, when many great men were adding them to their houses. It survived until 1647, but had been demolished by the 1680s.

During the sixteenth century there is no trace of any building activity, although a useful description of the Castle appears in a valuation of 1553:

Memorandum. Ther is a fyne manor place called the Castell of Hartylburye wherein the Byshop.... hath used oft tymes to lye, havinge ij lyttell towers covered with leade, and the chamber cauled the Byshop's chamber also covered with leade, and there is a chappell annexed to the said chamber lykewyse covered with lead...Also ther is a mote and a ponde adjoyning .....well stored with fyshe....

This is not a full description, for where are the Great Hall, kitchen and other rooms? But it does give a good picture of the roofs of the chapel and adjoining chamber with its lead roof. The two towers are the gate house and "Warwick's Tower", of which few details are known except that it stood at the south-east corner of the forecourt. In 1575 Queen Elizabeth paid a brief visit to Hartlebury during her stay in Worcestershire, but resided for most of the time at the Bishop's Palace in Worcester.

The Civil War made its own particular impact on the life of the Castle. Bishop Prideaux had identified himself with the Royalist cause and permitted the building to be garrisoned with one hundred and twenty men and twenty horses under Captain William Sandys. It was surrendered on 16th May 1646 "without a shot" under circumstances later regarded as suspicious and conditions which were not too carefully observed. The Bishop was deprived of his See and retired to Bredon to live with his son-in-law on a pittance of four shillings and sixpence a week, which he supplemented from time to time by selling personal goods. He died a poor man in 1650.

The Castle was valued in the Parliamentary Survey of 1647 which gives details of the materials in the Castle if it were to be demolished; fortunately it was decided that it would be more profitable to sell the property than to demolish it. The Survey listed the following rooms and outbuildings: hall, pantry, dining room over it, 15 by 18 feet, three little lodging chambers above that, kitchen, brewhouse of five bays, stables of five bays of low building, eight little houses 'built for soldiers hutts', Lady Willoughby's chamber, the Warwick Tower (ruinous), gate house tower of three chambers, decayed old stable, backhouse (probably meaning bakehouse), great chamber 39 x 21 feet (the Saloon), parlour 24 x 34 feet (now offices) and six little chambers next to the parlour. Obviously the Castle had not been demolished by the soldiers as is sometimes suggested, although the fences of the park were severely damaged.

The house, manor and land at Hartlebury were purchased for £3133.6s.8d. in 1648 by Thomas Westrow who reduced the Park to about half its original size. The Park associated with the Castle is referred to in the sixteenth century as about one mile "wherein be LXXVI Deare" and again in a deposition in the reign of Charles II in the seventeenth century as "a park of about 100 acres well stocked with deer, the Bishop paying the Rector in lieu of tythes one shoulder of every deer killed there". A detailed account of the deer in the Park from 1699-1709 was kept by the Bishop's secretary and is still preserved.

Thomas Westrow died in 1653 and at the Restoration in 1660 his children, obviously with a degree of self-interest, petitioned to keep the estate, on the grounds that 'the house is not fitt for the Bishop to live in (nor wilbee without the expence of manie hundreds of pounds, the castle being demolished in the time of the war)'. The damage was more the result of neglect than destruction, and the petition failed. The prediction concerning the cost of making the Castle habitable, however, proved correct and it was not until Bishop James Fleetwood came to the See in 1675 that any attempt was made to live again in the Castle. Bishop Morley (1660-62) was translated to Winchester and promised £500 towards repairing Hartlebury Castle if the work was begun within six months of his departure, and completed within two years. Morley was followed in rapid succession by Gauden (1662), Earle (1662/3), Skinner (1663/70) and Blandford (1671/75) who left £1,000 towards repairs, provided that Morley's money was forthcoming.

Fleetwood sued Blandford's executors (John Fell, Bishop of Oxford, and William Thomas, Dean of Worcester), and it would seem that he was successful.

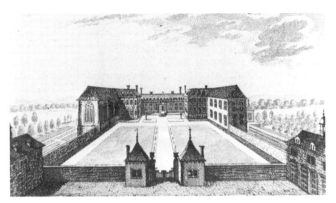

Buck's Print

Bishop Fleetwood's contribution to the remodelling of the Castle can be deduced from a set of accounts covering the years 1681/83, halfway through the work, which record that at least £450 was then spent. The only obvious trace of the works today is the coat of arms over the central porch. These accounts record a payment to Mr. Wood of Oxford for the completion of the coat of arms and for supplying drawings. He was the designer of all the new works, and was the Thomas Wood of Oxford (c1644/95), a master mason and sculptor, who undertook the stonework at the Palace at Oxford, then occupied by Bishop John Fell, one of those sued by Fleetwood to obtain the money for the work at Hartlebury.

Fleetwood completely rebuilt the north end of the Castle, creating an almost symmetrical elevation, balancing the chapel opposite. He installed mullion and transom (cross) windows everywhere except in the chapel, as can be seen in Buck's eighteenth century engraving. The grand staircase at the south end of the house was designed by Wood, and is identical in style to one he designed and built at the Old Ashmolean Museum in Oxford. The chapel was completely refitted in the latest style, with panelling, an altar rail with turned balusters, and a gallery, all made by two local joiners, John Powell and Reece Price. These chapel fittings were swept away in the eighteenth century.

He also replaced the low-pitched lead-covered chapel roof with one steep and tiled. Outside a new forecourt was laid out with two square plan lodges built by the bricklayers Thomas Hill and Thomas Wynnett using 76,000 bricks made in the park by John Jukes and John Giles. The lodges had pyramidal roofs with concave sides, capped by wrought-iron weather vanes, whilst the walls had a simple stone coping which is still preserved on the north wall, the other walls being reduced in the eighteenth century. The accounts

also show that Warwick's Tower was demolished. They do not mention filling in the moat to the east, or demolishing the gatehouse tower, which had probably already taken place. In 1683 Fleetwood died just as the works were completed, and his immediate successors did not choose to make Hartlebury their main home.

Bishop William Thomas who followed, died in 1689, and the inventory of his estate describes the building as consisting of:

> Hall, maids chamber, closet, Taylors chamber, Master Andrews chamber, my Lords chamber, the chamber at the stair head, the little parlour, Master Thomas chamber, the dining room, the pantry, the store house, chamber over the storehouse, the brewhouse, the kitchen, the dairy house, the lodge, the stable.

Only eleven or twelve of these, about a quarter of the total, were in the main house and so can only give a partial picture of the Castle at that time.

The biography of **Bishop John Hough** (1717/43), published in the year of his death states that:

> "He rebuilt so great a Part of the Episcopal Palace at Worcester, and made such improvements in his other Seat at Hartlebury, that...he expended....at least Seven Thousand Pounds. And these Schemes were executed with so nice a Judgement, that his Lordship has left little to be superadded by any of his Successors towards perfecting both those Episcopal Seats."

The work at Worcester consisted of the rebuilding of the new east front in 1719/23 at a cost of £1,164.16s.10d. As far as Hartlebury Castle was concerned Richard Hurd junior, writing in 1796 says that Hough 'rebuilt the Stables and Coach House and put Cupolas upon the roofs'. The coach houses which are visible in the foreground of Buck's print show the cupolas and a series of double doors along the front. They still stand today, that to the north containing the present offices of the County Museum and that to the south converted to dwellings. There is still a trace of the coach doors in the front wall of the southern building, that to the north was substantially rebuilt in the Edwardian period. Hough also remodelled the gardens. In a letter of 1731/2, he wrote:

> The Spring comes on in a most delightful manner; and old as I am, (about 81) I cannot forbear, after Winter's confinement, to peep out as the insects do, and see how the little improvements are carried on about me. My horses and carts have for some time never been at rest, from conveying earth to a low piece of ground, which by degree, we have gained from the moat; a tedious work, that makes no shew at present but of rubbish and disorder: yet I flatter myself that when it comes to be laid out into something of a regular

form, the idea of which is yet only in my head, my pains will not appear to be ill bestowed: for I shall then have above an acre of ground in a garden of a whimsical, and unusual but not disagreeable figure

This was the sunken garden to the south of the chapel in the filled-in moat. He also built the chimney stack in the Great Hall, although it is hard to imagine that it ever did much to heat that vast space. The overmantel bears his coat of arms in stone.

Bishop Isaac Maddox (1743/59) employed the brilliant young architect Henry Keene, twenty-two years old when work commenced, to redesign the chapel. This was done in the latest Gothick style in 1748/50, putting in plaster fan vaults, lining the walls with Gothick panelling and reconstructing the west screen with the gallery above. This end of the chapel is very reminiscent of the designs published by the architectural educator Batty Langley in his 'Ancient Architecture Restored and Improved by a Great Variety of Grand and Usefull Designs, entirely new, in the Gothick mode for the ornamentation of Buildings and Gardens', published in 1741/2.

The bishop's pew has an elaborate canopy supported on a number of slender wooden columns also designed by Henry Keene

but the wrought-iron Gothick altar rail was removed in the 1960s. Keene did not restrict himself to the fixtures, but designed furniture as well, four Gothick benches in the chapel, one of which is now in the ante-chamber, the fretted door and a cupboard for storing surplices with a Gothick ogee top. The chapel windows were entirely rebuilt, the east window with three lancets. The new glazing was designed by Dr. John Wall (an owner of the first Worcester porcelain factory, and early exploiter of Malvern water), but all that remains are some coats of arms reset in the side windows. The glazing of the east window was inserted in 1898 as a memorial to Bishop Henry Philpott (1861/91).

Maddox almost certainly added the octagonal Gothick cupola on the Hall roof with its ogee arches on the open sides and containing a bell. The east face of its plinth bears a dial linked to a weather vane to indicate wind direction. At the same time the lodges and the forecourt walls were Gothicised by adding crenellations.

East View

The stables rebuilt by Bishop Hough were adapted by Bishop Yeatman-Biggs for use as a college of clergy. Its use as such did not survive the war it being used then as the VAD Convalescent Hospital new offices of H & W County Museum.

The Palace of Worcester

Bishop James Johnson (1759/74) followed, and despite all this expenditure spent yet more money on the Castle. His chaplain (perhaps a little partisan) says that, 'The House, Offices, Fences and Park were in a very neglected and bad state; part of the House ruinous; which made it necessary for the present Bishop to repair every part of the buildings; and in most places he has much ornamented and improved it'. He inserted the sash windows, removing the old-fashioned mullion and transom windows, and gave the ground floor openings pointed heads. The dining room (now the Saloon) was lined to provide a smooth wall surface, and the elabo-

rate rococco decorations added, with ceiling panels bearing musical scores and wind instruments. The two decorative frames which flank the fireplace might have been designed to contain the portraits of George III and Queen Charlotte which now hang there. They came, however, from the Palace in Worcester in 1840, having been presented to Bishop Hurd by King George III after his visit to the Three Choirs Festival in 1788. The decorations have a further interest beyond their design, in that they are made of papier mache, a material only recently invented by Henry Clay of Birmingham.

In the Hall he altered the main staircase by adding a half landing and inserting a geometric staircase at the north end, cantilevered out from the wall without further support. He also altered the forecourt by changing the straight drive to a circular one.

Bishop Richard Hurd (1781/1808) succeeded Bishop Brownlow North and a picture of life at the Castle then is given by an inventory which gives some details of the house and its furnishings, hardly any of which are still at the Castle. Forty rooms in the main buildings are listed, as well as sundry passages, lofts and outbuildings. The principal rooms were in the south wing and included the dressing room, complete with all necessary comforts, such as tea kettle stand, six French arm chairs and two blue festoon curtains at the windows. This is now the bishop's study which in 1781 was in the adjoining room, now a small sitting room for the bishop. The State Rooms, then in everyday use, included the eating parlour (Saloon), the drawing room (now divided into offices), the breakfast room (the present entrance hall of the bishop's house) and the long gallery which ran behind the Hall. It was not the grand long gallery of so many great houses, but rather a large passage constructed in the seventeenth century, well furnished with framed prints, busts on pedestals, some stained glass in the windows and a mahogany billiard table. The Great Hall itself was very sparsely furnished, reflecting how little it was used.

The inventory then moves to the lower end of the Hall, where the servants had been housed since the medieval period. Here were the servants' rooms and the main kitchen, with all the utensils listed. The servants' rooms ran from the maids' garret (with four poster beds) to the housekeeper's room, in which soap, candles, cheese, dried fruit and sugar are itemised, presumably for safekeeping. Out-houses included a dairy, laundry, brewhouse and stables. The contents of the Castle were valued at £1,264.12s.2d., compared with a mere £221.18s.6d. for the goods at the Palace in Worcester.

Bishop Hurd made the last major addition to the Castle, the finest architectural feature of the building, a library built in 1782 to house his large book collection. It lies at the rear of the Hall, with the entrance from the main staircase, is built over the seventeenth century long gallery to a design by an obscure archi-

Top left: Princes Room showing earlier bold bamboo patterned wallpaper. *Centre and right:* Chapel. *Bottom:* The Hurd Library.

Top: The Great Hall   *Centre:* The Long Gallery
Bottom: Saloon

tect, James Smith of Shropshire, and consists of one main space with an ante-chamber at each end, and a bay window thrown out to the west to overlook the moat. The ante-chambers and bay window are each defined by a screen with two Ionic columns. The long west wall is filled by sash windows, whilst the east wall has a central fireplace flanked by two bookcases, each of five bays, the larger central bay with a scrolled pediment. The delicate plaster ceiling was executed by Joseph Bromfield of Shrewsbury and the coved frieze is decorated with a series of portrait medallions of writers admired by Hurd, including Alexander Pope, which alternate with various classical motifs, and one or two non-classical items such as a crozier and mitre. The centre of the ceiling is broken by a shallow dome. The wooden columns are marbled, the walls painted white and the bookcases grained light brown, the original intention, as shown in the contemporary design, being to paint the walls pale green and the bookcases white.

The Gothick lodge by the main road was probably built by Hurd for the deeds show it to have been erected in about 1781. He also built 'The Shrubbery' in 1783, a house on the opposite side of the Stourport road, for his spinster sister. It is said that they did not find living together "convenient".

Hurd was a close friend of the Royal Family and in 1807 the Prince of Wales paid a brief visit to the Castle. The room fitted out for that occasion, now known as the Prince's Room (formerly the Prince Regent's Room) still retains some of the furniture from that time. The elegant bed has the Prince of Wales's feathers painted on the tester (canopy), and these are repeated on the window pelmet. The bed retains its original hangings, but sadly the contemporary bold bamboo pattern wallpaper has been removed since the 1930s and replaced by a pale paper. A fragment of the original is preserved on a screen and a picture of the room taken in 1931 shows the pattern clearly.

Almost all the rest of the furnishings in the house were imported in 1844 from the Palace in Worcester, when it was sold to the Dean and Chapter for use as the Deanery. The 'Chinese Chippendale' chairs now in the Library were at Worcester, as can be seen in a drawing of about 1820, as well as the two seventeenth century refectory tables in the Great Hall, said to be those made for Bishop Morley, but since shortened.

There have been no major additions since Hurd's day. The Castle was made the only official residence of the bishop in 1846. In the 1960s the bishop's lodgings were reduced to the south wing only, the State Rooms were passed to a Trust and the service end of the house became the home of the newly formed County Museum. The changes involved blocking up a few doorways and dividing the long gallery into several manageable rooms for the bishop's family. The continuity of residence by the bishop at Hartlebury, however, was retained, at a time when even demolition was seriously considered as a solution, and this part of the story comes later (p.35).

BISHOPS OF WORCESTER.

680-1535 *by Kevin Down.*

The Diocese of Worcester was founded in 680 as part of the reorganisation of the English Church by Archbishop Theodore of Canterbury to be the bishopric of the kingdom of the Hwicce; its cathedral church of Saint Peter was built at the capital, Worcester, and the diocese had more or less the same boundaries as the Hwiccan kingdom: most of Worcestershire and Gloucestershire and a large part of south Warwickshire. By the end of the seventh century the bishopric had begun building up its estates - Hartlebury was probably acquired in the third quarter of the ninth century - and by the time of the Norman Conquest, the Church of Worcester was lord of much of the land in the three counties. The first bishop, Bosel, came from Saint Hilda's monastery at Whitby and was consecrated by Archbishop Theodore in 680. On his resignation in 691 he was succeeded, after the short pontificate of Ostfor, by Saint Egwin (693-7ll), the founder of Evesham Abbey. He resigned in 711 to become abbot of that house, by his action giving it a spurious claim to special status because the saint had preferred the abbey to the bishopric.

In the second half of the tenth century the See was occupied by two of the leading reformers of the English Church, who introduced a reformed Benedictine monasticism from the Continent, Saint Dunstan (Worcester 957-9 and Canterbury 960-88) and Saint Oswald (961-92).

Oswald's pontificate was particularly formative for the See because he reformed his own cathedral chapter in 969 by introducing to it, with some difficulty, monks to replace its secular canons, and at the same time he built, near the old cathedral of Saint Peter, a new monastic church of Saint Mary for them. To help finance this new establishment Oswald used his influence with King Edgar to increase greatly the lands of the Church of Worcester. The later "Life" stresses his fine physique, magnificent singing voice, accessible and attractive character, his love of the poor, his preaching and pastoral zeal. From 972 he held Worcester in plurality with the underendowed See of York, thus bringing Worcester within York's sphere of influence; in this some of his successors followed him, notably Wulstan I (1003-16), the celebrated homilist.

Ealdred (1046-62) combined Worcester with Hereford and would have added York to them had not Pope Nicholas II's disapproval compelled him to resign Worcester. As bishop he was required to fight Irish pirates and their Welsh allies, not always successfully, and he is perhaps best remembered for his defence of the monastic precinct at Worcester by his cursing Urse d'Abitot, the Conqueror's sheriff of Worcestershire. On his translation to York, he was succeeded by Wulstan II (1062-95), Saint Wulstan, perhaps the greatest occupant of the See.

Wulstan, a Warwickshire man, monk and prior of Worcester, was the last survivor of the old English hierarchy, kept on by William the Conqueror perhaps because of his prompt submission, his enthusiasm for the Gregorian Reform and the known sanctity of his life; here at least was one English saint about whom the Normans had no doubt. By his survival he was able to maintain on the whole the rights and possessions of his See and skilfully set the foundations of its later prosperity by guiding it through a period of crisis. As a monk he had been zealous in pastoral works, preaching, baptising and giving advice, work which he continued after his consecration, carefully visiting his diocese by covering a set area each year and confirming such crowds that he was occupied from dawn to dusk. In keeping with his enthusiasm for reform, he strongly opposed the slave trade, of which there was an important centre in his diocese at Bristol, and enforced the rules of clerical celibacy with the rigorist insistance that married priests should make the choice between their wives and their churches. At the same time he enhanced the setting of the Church's worship by his encouragement of church-building, the provision of stone altars and, his most enduring achievement in this field, the rebuilding of the cathedral, beginning with the present crypt in 1084. He was canonized by Pope Innocent III in 1203 and his shrine became the centre of a flourishing cult.

Samson (1096-1115), Wulstan's successor, provided a stark contrast with him; he was all that the Hildebrandine Church abhorred: the son of a priest, both brother and father of an Archbishop of York (both called Thomas), of worldly tastes and habits - William of Malmesbury, admittedly no friend, says that he was over-addicted to the pleasures of the table. As a royal clerk, whose final loyalty was to the king, he may have been the compiler of the Domesday Book; Worcester was perhaps his reward. Samson rather than Wulstan set the pattern for the twelfth century, though some of his successors were more edifying; for example, Roger of Gloucester (1164-79), youngest son of Robert, Earl of Gloucester, and grandson of Henry I. An upholder of Church rights and friend of Saint Thomas Becket, despite his origins, he strongly opposed nepotism in the Church and the enrichment of his own relatives out of its revenues.

In the aftermath of the fourth Lateran Council (1215), in an atmosphere of reform, the English Church possibly possessed the most distinguished group of bishops of any between the Norman Conquest and the Reformation, men who showed a high level of character, learning and efficiency, combined with a fervent belief in the ideals of Pope Innocent III and his reforming predecessors. Such a bishop was William of Blois (1218-36) who, in his efforts to reform his clergy, issued an important set of constitutions covering many aspects of Church life. He is probably best remembered now as the bishop who laid the foundation stone of the new east end of the cathedral in 1224. His work was continued during the long episcopates of his successors Walter de Cantelupe (1236-66) and Godfrey Giffard (1268-1302), both members of important baronial families and both schooled in royal service, circumstances to which they owned their promotion.

Cantelupe was the model of a reforming diocesan; he carefully visited his diocese, ordered the life of his subjects, clerical and lay, issued documents on a wide variety of matters and promulgated a celebrated collection of constitutions at his Worcester synod in 1240 which became a model for later legislators. Clearly a man of the firmest principle and a robust defender of the rights of his See against all comers, and particularly against monasteries, he was nevertheless capable too of diplomatic compromise and it was during his time that the old quarrel between the bishop and Evesham Abbey about rights in the Vale of Evesham churches was finally settled. Reputed to be one of the 'friends of the Pope' in England, like Grosseteste, he was fully prepared to oppose papal designs on English benefices. It is not entirely surprising that in the troubles between Henry III and his barons, Cantelupe took the side of baronial reform in its attempts to impose limitations on the king's actions and became a staunch supporter and close friend of Simon de Montfort, whom he entertained at his manor of Kempsey before the Battle of Evesham in 1265. For this support of the baronial opposition he was excommunicated and suspended from his See by the papal legate, though he was allowed to retire to his manor at Blockley, where he died in February 1266. One of the greatest bishops of his time and uncle of a saint, Thomas of Hereford, it was said that only his support of Simon de Montfort stood in the way of his own canonization.

After Cantelupe, undoubted royalists were appointed to Worcester, first Nicholas of Ely, Chancellor of England for eighteen months before his translation to Winchester; then Godfrey Giffard for thirty-four years.

Giffard is the first Bishop of Worcester who is known to have kept a register, which survives, to show up in detail how he governed his diocese, healed the upsets caused there by the baronial wars, and coped with the growing demands of ecclesiastical and estate administration. Personally he seems to have been a tough character, a rigorous superior and a fierce opponent, as well as a very grand prelate, who in his will bequeathed much jewellery, silver plate, silk vestments and armour and who travelled with so large an entourage that it required, according to the hostile Worcester chronicler, one hundred and forty horses. Possibly it was this grandeur of taste as much as defensive considerations which led him in 1268 to obtain licences to crenellate his manor houses of Hartlebury and Withington and his palace at Worcester and to complete the fortification of Hartlebury which Cantelupe had begun unofficially around 1255. In the process he turned just another manor house into a palace which was to become one of the most important residences of the bishops during the rest of the Middle Ages and the moats and ponds of Hartlebury as well as the remaining work in the palace at Worcester give some idea of the magnificence of his conception. They are a fitting memorial to a man who seems to lack the earnest high-mindedness of Walter de Cantelupe and who, although a conscientious diocesan, nevertheless in some ways points towards the increasingly secular outlook of many of the later medieval bishops.

After the long and distinguished pontificates of Bishop Cantelupe and Bishop Giffard, only three of the twenty-seven bishops between 1302 and 1535 could aspire to comparably long tenures of the See: Henry Wakefield (1375-95), John Carpenter (1444-76) and the mostly absent Silvestro de' Gigli (1498-1521). Worcester, therefore, probably because it was not one of the richer Sees, became a somewhat transitional diocese, for many of its occupants merely a stepping-stone to higher things; Ely (four times), London, York, Canterbury (thrice), and even the Papacy in the case of Cardinal Giulio de' Medici (1521-22), who, as Clement VII, was the only bishop of an English diocese to become Pope. Worcester was not unusual in this and this situation was largely a reflection of the sort of man who became a bishop and how he came to the See. Most owed their promotion to the king, usually as a reward for services, administrative, political, medical, or even, as the author of the Vita Edwardi II says of Bishop Reynolds (1308-13), theatrical:

Clement VII

19

"in theatrical games he held the first place, and through this he gained the king's favour." Perhaps his was a talent for charades and maybe he should have some of the blame for that monarch's inadequacies. He ended his days at Canterbury, having spent little time in the Diocese of Worcester. Most of these bishops either had had careers in royal service or were given the diocese to support them in an important office of state. As a result, many were of a political and secular outlook, John Wyclif's "Caesarian clergy". Not untypical was Philip Morgan (1419-26), a diplomat who tried to combine pastoral zeal in the diocese with a career in diplomacy and assiduous attendance at Henry VI's small council. Similarly John Alcock (1476-86), founder of Jesus College, Cambridge, was kept from the concerns of his See by the preoccupations of office as president of the Prince of Wales's council, during which time he ordained for the Diocese of Worcester at Ludlow Castle by licence of the Bishop of Hereford. Perhaps the ultimate absentees were the four Italian bishops (1497-1535), for whom the income of the See was maintenance for royal ambassadors in Rome.

Akin to the preceding group were the nobles: Thomas Cobham (1317-27), of the well-known Kentish family, and Simon de Montacute (1334-37), a relation of the Earl of Salisbury; both, however, were active in diocesan affairs. Less so were the later nobles, Richard Clifford (1404-07) and Thomas Bourchier (1435-43). Bourchier was the grandest of the late medieval bishops, son of Anne, Countess of Eu, and a great-grandson of Edward III, a connection which undoubtedly made him bishop at the uncanonically early age of twenty-eight and eventually saw him elevated to Canterbury. A doctor of theology, many of his acts are dated at Oxford, of which he was Chancellor, or London, though he spent some time in his diocese each year and held ordinations in the chapels at Alvechurch Manor and Hartlebury Castle in the mid-1430s.

Members of religious orders tended to be more concerned with ecclesiastical affairs. An exception was William Gainsborough (1302-07), a Franciscan lecturer in divinity at Oxford, Edward I's ambassador to France and reader in theology at the palace of Pope Boniface VIII, who provided him to Worcester, from which he was frequently absent on the king's service. Wulstan de Bransford (1339-49), possibly from Bransford and the son of a citizen of Worcester, monk of the cathedral priory and prior from 1317, became bishop as the result of a genuine free election. Well versed in diocesan affairs before becoming bishop because he had served as vicar general for his predecessors, he was solely concerned throughout his episcopate with the pastoral care of his charge both through regular administration and, in spite of ill health from early in his rule, assiduous visitation. During his ten years he was absent for only a few weeks and his register is accordingly one of the biggest in the Worcester series. He died at Hartlebury Castle on 6th August 1349 when the Black Death was at its height in the diocese.

The two remaining essentially religious bishops were both royal nominees rewarded for services: Robert Tideman of Winchcombe (1395-1401), Cistercian abbot of Beaulieu and doctor to Richard II to whom he remained faithful to the end. The second was Thomas Peverell (1407-19), a Carmelite friar, like Tideman translated from Llandaff to Worcester, but for supporting Henry IV who deposed Richard II. He is possibly best remembered for his condemnation of John Badby of Evesham as an incorrigible heretic in the Carnary Chapel of the cathedral in 1409.

Henry Wakefield (1375-95) **and John Carpenter** (1444-76), who enjoyed two of the longer tenures of the See, stand out for devotion to episcopal work and continual residence, surprisingly because their backgrounds did not augur well for their subsequent careers as pastoral bishops. Wakefield rose through the civil service. After the death of Edward III, of whose will he was an executor, he returned to his diocese in March 1378 and devoted himself to its work, living mainly at Hartlebury and Alvechurch. Carpenter had two possible distractions because, in addition to being a king's clerk and chaplain between 1430 and 1441, he was also a distinguished university figure, a doctor of theology of Oxford, Provost of Oriel and later Chancellor of the University. Contrary to expectations, he proved to be, by fifteenth century standards, an enthusiastic pastoral and resident bishop, greatly concerned with the life of the diocese and for the temporal and spiritual well-being of his people. Founder of libraries at the Carnary Chapel in Worcester and the Calendaries in Bristol and founder of Westbury College, he added more than most to the plant of the See.

The role of the Medieval Bishop

The foregoing accounts of late medieval occupants of the See of Worcester have pointed out that some were determined residents while others were assiduous absentees. The implication is perhaps too strongly made that the former are much to be preferred to the latter from a pastoral point of view. In reality, the difference between these two types of bishop was not strongly marked. Inspection of their registers does not reveal great differences between them and to a large extent this was due to the convention about what a bishop was and how he was expected to behave. Although the bishop was required to be concerned about the spiritual and temporal welfare of his subjects, the modern bishop's close pastoral involvement in the life of the diocese was not the late medieval custom, whatever pastoral theologians might have advised. Generally it was the administrative, jurisdictional and punitive side of his task which was emphasized, together with the seeking out and correcting aspect, as he sought the regular provision of religious services and the moral reformation of his clergy and laity, so that the relationship with his clerical and lay subjects was more that of distant ruler and judge who descended occasionally on visitation and whose court provided sanctions for misbehaviour. Accordingly it is likely that many people never saw their own bishop, unless they lived near one of his palaces, or by one of the main routes around the diocese or to London, or near one of the central churches where he made his visitations.

Another bar to efficiency in pastoral concern was provided by his being an important landholder who inevitably, therefore, became caught up, whether he liked it or not, in the problems of estate management, local government, and the other concerns of great magnates. Government regarded bishops as great men who were needed to preserve the temporal order and to help with various tasks of government, such as attendance at the king's council and diplomacy, as well as frequent involvement in politics, often the result of their connections with the Crown or great men to whose parties they often belonged. Inevitably many tended to be preoccupied with secular matters and government and to be political and worldly in outlook. In the eyes of ordinary people they were very much part of the political establishment and were allied with the forces of government. A good example of this in Worcester was Bishop John Alcock, who devoted himself almost exclusively to his position as tutor to Edward, Prince of Wales (the elder of the Princes in the Tower) at Ludlow, which was the focal point for the exercise of royal authority in Wales, the Marches and adjacent shires. Close acquaintance with and supervision of his charge was made even more difficult in many dioceses by their very size; they were too large - Worcester was about seventy miles long by about forty-five wide, stretching from Birmingham to Bristol, from the Malverns to Edge Hill. This was why bishops needed centres throughout their dioceses to allow them stopping off points on their long journeys.

The Bishop's Principal Pastoral Concerns were first, the regular provision of Mass and the sacraments in every parish by ensuring an adequate clergy and the upkeep of church buildings; the supervision of lay morals, behaviour and belief, including the extirpation of heresy; and the supervision of religious houses. He did this first of all by his sacramental and spiritual functions: ordaining priests, consecrating altars and churches and confirming the laity. Exercising his jurisdiction he examined and instituted clergy to livings and tried to ensure adequate support for them. Lay and clerical discipline was dealt with through the process of visitation and the activities of the bishop's court. It was usual to hold a primary visitation after enthronement, a slow progress on horseback with a retinue through the diocese, deanery by deanery, meeting both clergy and laity at one central church, confirming and consecrating altars and churches in each deanery. It was not necessarily uninterrupted; Bishop Bransford on his primary visitation in 1339 spent from 14th October to 19th November on the Archdeaconry of Worcester, often staying at his manors in the area:

Blockley, Tredington, Hampton. Then by 25th November he was back at Hartlebury Castle well in time for Christmas and no doubt to catch up on other day-to-day administration. Early in February he was back on the road, beginning the visitation of the Archdeaconry of Gloucester at Beckford on 7th February. Again it was interrupted, this time probably for Easter at Hartlebury, and he finished eventually late in June. After the visitation, the findings were dealt with and injunctions were sent out to remedy faults. Subsequent visitations were supposed to be held every three years, but there is very little evidence that this was in fact done, though it may be that the records have not survived. In many cases bishops did not complete a visitation themselves, but delegated their powers to a deputy; indeed all the visitations of the Italian bishops in the sixteenth century were of necessity carried out in this way by their vicars general.

When not on visitation, the bishop had much regular administration to occupy him and his clerks: institutions of clergy to benefices, the granting of licences, sending out mandates on all manner of subjects. Some, like Adam Orleton, acted from a variety of their manors; others, like Wakefield, did not move around a great deal and preferred to spend most of their time ruling from their northern palaces at Hartlebury and Alvechurch, which were good centres for much of the diocese. Carpenter was unusual in spending a great deal of his time in the vicinity of Bristol. Orleton, who spent more than half his episcopate away from the diocese, performed many of his tasks including ordinations and consecrating the holy oils at his manor of Beaumes in Berkshire and at various places in France. Worcester and the palace there were visited fairly infrequently, for major feasts, ordinations, and the Chrism Mass on Maundy Thursday and at the beginning of a visitation; but bishops generally preferred their rural manors.

How important was this frequent absence by many bishops? Given the expected activities of the typical late medieval diocesan, absence was probably not very important because he usually kept control over its affairs from wherever he was, as Orleton did from France, and also because in his absence his functions were carried out more or less adequately by deputies. For liturgical tasks which required someone in episcopal orders, assistant bishops, often called suffragans, were appointed, commonly occupants of Irish Sees or religious and others who held such Sees *in partibus infidelium* as Nazareth, Sidon or Tenos. The administrative and jurisdictional functions were exercised by vicars general, officials principal, commissaries and others who were usually the bishop's chief helpers when he was in his diocese. The system of deputies coped completely during the pontificates of the four Italian bishops between 1497 and 1535 when the rule of the diocese passed almost entirely to a series of permanent vicars general who acted under the distant supervision of the leading member of the government in London, Bishop Fox, Cardinal Wolsey or Thomas Cromwell.

LIFE AT HARTLEBURY CASTLE

What sort of life did medieval bishops lead? Their contemporaries equated bishops in society with earls, and prelates by and large conducted themselves as great lords, splendid magnates, rather than austere churchmen. This begins with their living in palaces and important manor houses. Although, as at Hartlebury, often called castles and crenellated, their dwellings usually are more redolent of the palace than the fortress, and are perhaps better described as country houses; indeed some bishops clearly used Hartlebury as a retreat from their more regular concerns. Like most great noblemen, bishops were enthusiastic about hunting and kept parks at their major residences, including Hartlebury. In his palaces the bishop kept great state and lived with a large household, and when he went abroad he travelled with a numerous retinue. The impression given by all this was not entirely edifying, as appears by the reaction of the mystic Margery Kempe (c. 1373 - c. 1440) to Bishop Peverell's retinue when she encountered some of its members at his manor of Henbury in 1417. Margery met one of the bishop's "worthiest men" in town and he took her to the bishop's hall while the bishop himself was still in bed; there she was clearly startled by what she saw; "When she came into the hall, she saw many of the Bishop's men in clothes very fashionably slashed and cut into points. Lifting up her hand, she blessed herself. And then they said to her, 'What the devil's wrong with you?' She replied, 'Whose men are you?' They answered, 'The Bishop's men.' Then she said, 'No, truly, you are more like the devil's men'." These men were probably the company which escorted the bishop when he travelled or perhaps young men living in as part of their education and who also took a part in the running of his household, for a bishop's life, like that of an earl, would be lived according to elaborate ceremony. The bishop would be served on bended knee with elaborate and lengthy ritual, he would eat alone or with exalted persons and be attended by men of high social status, sometimes in his hall, but by the later Middle Ages probably more often in his great chamber. There would, too, have been an equally impressive liturgical routine centred on the chapel and performed by the bishop's chaplains.

This sort of life required a large and varied staff, details of which are given from time to time in the bishops' registers and financial accounts throughout the period, though no Bishop of Worcester aspired to the household of five hundred attributed to Cardinal Wolsey by George Cavendish; by the general standards of earls, their households may have been on the modest side, in Bishop Bourgchier's case perhaps in the region of twenty persons. In this household the clerical establishment included the clerks and priests of the chapel, the domestic chaplains and perhaps an almoner. There were also close clerical attendants whom Bishop Reynolds referred to as "our clerks and table fellows", some of whom were occasionally relatives of the bishop. These were his closest associates, well rewarded and provided with robes and furs and their keep with the bishop himself. From time to time their number would be augmented by members of the bishop's council, which sometimes met at Hartlebury, perhaps in the "principal chamber", or by officers of his court of audience, which sat there on occasions in the chapel, and by his great clerks like the chancellor and registrar. Documents issued in the household would be written by the bishop's scribe. In addition to the clerical establishment there were secular servants who are mentioned from time to time in documents: the constable, the bishop's valet, the barber, the cook, the janitor, messengers, a runner to carry messages, and possibly a tailor who made up into liveries the large amounts of cloth bought for the purpose by bishops.

Feeding such a household must have been a formidable operation and required considerable resources. In the 1430s under Bishop Bourgchier everyday running costs were divided between eight departments of the household and amounted to about three hundred pounds a year, the equivalent of roughly a third of the annual income of the See. Of this sum about a third went to the provision of meat and fish for the kitchen; ale in the buttery (at a rate of a gallon a person a day) and wine in the cellar accounted for

St Wulstan Malvern Priory
1062-1095

Latimer 1535-39

Heath 1543-51 and 1553-55

Whitgift 1577-83

Bilson 1596-97

a quarter, together making the major part of the total expenditure. Bourgchier's household was not unique in its consumption of wine; in 1312 Bishop Reynolds laid down at Hartlebury Castle a large consignment of wine which he had bought at Worcester for £24.12s.1d. and Bishop Wakefield, later in the century, spent £33 on wine at Bristol for his manor of Henbury. Other expenditure was on bread (the pantry), spices, candles (the chandlery), fuel for the hall and fodder for the stables. On top of this were the servants' wages and the laundry bill. Bought provisions were probably supplemented by local produce, for example, venison, the fruit of hunting in the park, and hay from the bishop's meadow at Hartlebury.

An idea of the magnificence of the episcopal household is strongly conveyed by Bishop Bourgchier's purchases of 1435/6 at the beginning of his pontificate. As well as horses with their saddles and other equipment, the usual pots and pans, chests, blankets and a great deal of clothing, the bishop bought silver dishes, saucers, chargers, basins, candelabra, rings and seals. The same state is reflected in Bishop Wakefield's will of 1395 in which he bequeathed a lot of plate silver dishes, saucers and pots, his basin and ewer, silver spoons, covered cups, both silver and gilt, and his no doubt magnificent bed with the eagles. Supporting this way of life was a substantial income from the lands of the See, broad estates organised into fifteen manors scattered around Worcestershire, Gloucestershire and South Warwickshire, run by another group of officers, which produced an income of about £1,200 around 1300 and between £900 and £1,074 in the early sixteenth century.

This picture of the Bishops of Worcester in the later Middle Ages perhaps stresses the similarities between the bishops and the great secular magnates to the detriment of their lives as churchmen and to some extent this is an inevitable consequence of modern awareness of the incongruity between the great state they kept up and the essential nature of their vocation. On the whole, the bishops themselves seem to have been unaware of these inconsistencies and found no great problem in dividing their attention between the spiritual and the temporal; and in fairness to them it must be said that even in the midst of secular preoccupations they were generally of upright personal life and concerned about their spiritual responsibilities, even if, on occasions they were on the seamier side of politics. So, in addition to their normal episcopal duties, they are found to be solicitous to some extent about care for the poor and for their tenants, for public works like roads and bridges, for church building and education. Taken as a group, they lack the distinction as pastoral bishops of some earlier occupants of the See but they bear comparison with most of their contemporaries in the other dioceses of England.

1535 to 1860 *by Dr. B.S. Benedikz*

When the Reformation came to Worcester, it came very thoroughly - in all its aspects. It must be admitted that Worcester diocese needed a fresh gale of the Spirit to blow through it, for it had been the milch-cow assigned by Henry VII and Henry VIII to their 'spokesmen' in Rome, providing these men with status and stipend without exacting any diocesan duties in return. But when Henry VIII chose to get rid of Chirolamo Ghinucci (1522-1534) from Worcester, he replaced him with almost the last man to be a natural successor to such a prelate.

Hugh Latimer (1535-1539) was to be the first of the 'men of principle' who were to adorn Worcester at intervals over the next century. No one could call him a 'career cleric' or 'court cleric' such as his predecessors, but in one way he recalls Walter Cantelupe - when he made up his mind he remained true to his convictions without reservations, no matter what the cost. By 1535, when he was fifty years old, he had been for ten years a definite and devout leader of the Reformation party in King Henry's church - a thorough scholar, especially in the Scriptures, and utterly devoted to the ideal which he expressed in a memorable phrase "for the preaching of the word of God unto the people is called meat ... it is meat, it is no dainties".

Prideaux 1641-1650

Stillingfleet 1689-1699

Maddox 1743-1759

Hurd 1781-1808

Carr 1831-1841

At Cambridge, where he was for many years a Fellow of Clare Hall, he became one of the champions of Church Reformation who came forward as the original proponents were silenced - and in Latimer the English Church received her golden-tongued preacher, as in Cranmer she found her inspired liturgist. Latimer was no political revolutionary: he obeyed the King's call to take up the bishopric, he came as soon as duties would let him to Worcester, and his register shows him to be a dutiful and hard-working diocesan during his four short years at Hartlebury. During this time his political backer, Thomas Cromwell, organised the first round of despoliation of monastic houses in England: Latimer seems to have supported this without qualms, though he was not happy with the King's shift in theology after he had been disappointed in the Protestant Queen Anne Boleyn (Latimer's patroness), had lost Queen Jane in childbirth and was finding Continental Protestants no help with his own problems.

Latimer had thrown in his lot with the Lutheran side of the Reforming party, which placed Scripture above all other guides to faith and so caused consternation in conservative circles, where the Bible had held a low place in contemporary theology, and his view of the monastic world was a very low one. But in the end Latimer's honesty made him a useless tool for the devious ends of King Henry and his ministers, and he was not entirely displeased to resign his See (even though one biographer has suggested that he was manoeuvred into doing so) and to return to the simple preaching of Scriptural supremacy for Christian faith and life.

There is evidence that, when Edward VI's regents dispossessed Bishop Heath, an effort was made to get him to return to Worcester, but it is clear that he resisted this attempt in order to retain his freedom as preacher and teacher. It is no surprise, therefore, that when Queen Mary's reign brought back the most conservative form of religion, Latimer, the outspoken advocate of reform for thirty years, was among the first to be tackled by the new authorities. He had been an obedient servant to King Henry, accepting the bishopric offered, but he had characteristically treated it as a bishopric of souls, not of state, and had laid it down with relief in order to keep more freely to his principles in practice. Now he was prepared to be Queen Mary's faithful subject in the state, but there was no question of his returning to a religious allegiance which he had cast off thirty years before as a matter of principle after much thought and prayer. The fiercest efforts of Mary's inquisitors failed to shake him and so, at seventy, Latimer went to his death with the same upright courage that he had shown in his lifetime, leaving behind the words of encouragement which encouraged the shrinking Bishop Ridley by his side at the stake.

"Be of good courage, Master Ridley and play the man. We shall this day light such a candle by God's grace in England, as (I trust) shall never be put out."

After Latimer's departure, and the short stay of the Civil Service-trained but dull John Bell, who also resigned his See after four years, Henry was clearly in need of a trusted and experienced man to preside over the senior See of Worcester. As a result of the making of Gloucestershire into the Sees of Gloucester and Bristol, the diocese was now concentrated on Worcestershire and, apart from his London house and The Old Palace in Worcester, the Bishops of Worcester made Hartlebury Castle their home. To this reduced See now came Nicolas Heath, translated from Rochester.

In **Bishop Heath** (1543-51 & 1553-55) we meet one of the best representatives of the conservative party in Henry VIII's church. His career up to January 1544 can be matched by that of a whole host of older bishops from Hugh of Blois onwards; it is what happened afterwards which makes him remarkable among the inhabitants of Hartlebury. He lacked the sheer status of Latimer - perhaps the greatest incumbent of the See after St. Oswald - but he had two especial qualities which have been the common property of all those who have held that See worthily - qualities which have enabled them to work much for its blessing in good years, and to give the only acceptable lead in bad years. These were the qualities of sureness of conviction, and largeness of heart; qualities found in full force in Hugh Latimer, but in Heath coloured more gently by his different training, and resulting in different reactions to different challenges.

A conservative, Heath was no less obedient to King Henry's call to a bishopric than the older man, and yet he must have been very conscious of the dangers of succeeding to the See of the only member of the episcopate brave enough to withstand King Henry to the end, for John Fisher had been only four years dead and his service of thirty-one years at Rochester must have been still fresh in men's memories, since Bishop John Hilsey was by all accounts as unmemorable a man at Rochester as John Bell (1539-1543) had been at Worcester. Yet there is no record of trouble in Heath's day in Rochester diocese such as bedevilled London in the days of Bishops Stokesley and Bonner, and when Heath moved in at Hartlebury he does not seem to have changed his approach, for John Oswyn, a printer of determinedly Protestant leanings, was left alone, and there is no record of Bishop Heath sending out inquisitors in the manner of Bonner of London or (later) Baynes of Coventry to sniff out heretics in his diocese.

Nonetheless, where Heath knew his mind he was resolute. Over an ordinal he could not accept, he would not budge, and in 1549-52 he and John Day, Bishop of Chichester, resisted the Edwardine liturgy to the point of imprisonment and deprivation, as numerous public documents make clear. Again, like Latimer, Heath was willing not to oppose the King's directive, but he was also equally determined not to endorse it with his signature if he could not do so in conscience. Accordingly, John Hooper, Bishop of Gloucester, was intruded by the Crown into the See of Worcester, and the two bishoprics reunited, but this was only to last for a year, since the Protestant King Edward died on 6th July 1553 and with his elder sister the conservatives of the English Church took command again. Out of their prisons came the aged Tunstall of Durham, Heath of Worcester and Day of Chichester to resume the government of their Sees. Not that Heath was to stay for long, for when a year later Archbishop Holgate of York was deprived for having married, he was duly promoted, and served at York as he had served at Worcester, without rancour and without persecuting his opponents. Once again, however, when Queen Elizabeth reintroduced vernacular liturgy and with it the Edwardine ordinal which had been the testing point of his previous encounter with the civil authorities, Heath did not fail. Rather than betray his deepest convictions he gave up his preferments and retired into private life.

Unlike Edward's regents, Elizabeth clearly thought well of the deprived Archbishop, for he was provided with an income and a home in a Surrey manor-house and there he remained for the last twenty years of his life, gently determined not to accept the new Church regime, but equally an entirely loyal subject to the Queen, refusing to have anything to do with political treason. Elizabeth's appreciation of this may be seen by her action at the most delicate time of all, when Pope Sixtus V issued a bull releasing her subjects from all allegiance to the Queen. In the same year she came openly and paid the ex-Archbishop a visit which (though no doubt a costly privilege to Dr. Heath!) enabled him to show his unshaken loyalty to the Queen's person in such a way as to dissociate himself from the plotters who thereafter began to seek her life.

John Whitgift Master of Trinity College, Cambridge, was consecrated to the See of Worcester shortly before Heath's death (in 1579). In Latimer and Heath we have looked at two men whose principles led them to refuse to serve the Church under a government opposed to their own tenets: in Whitgift (1577-1583) we find a man no less firmly principled, but one for whom the settlement of Elizabeth was the embodiment of his principles. His career through the University of Cambridge had involved him in intense disputation with religious extremists, and his need to define and set out his standpoint in print meant that when he came to Worcester he knew what he believed, and this was what the Queen's ecclesiastical settlement had provided: a strong, reformed episcopate and a liturgy reformed and available to the people, reverent and orderly, with doctrine and ritual alike based on Scripture and the teaching of the Fathers of the Church that developed from Scripture. Over his six years at Worcester and twenty-one years at Canterbury he held as fearlessly to his principles as his predecessors had to theirs - with this difference, that where they had eventually to confront a secular government hostile to their own tenets, Whitgift had to steer a government divided within itself on Church policy, and in that task he

had the unwavering support of Queen Elizabeth who, having once taken to him, came to trust him as she trusted no other man, for in her dying hours she clung to the hand of him whom she had in jest called her "little black husband". And, as he had served the Church under Elizabeth, so Whitgift lived to see her secure passage into the reign of King James. Much maligned by enemies to whom truth was visibly a stranger - probably because he refused to give way before their blustering and deliberate blackmail - John Whitgift had in due measure the qualities which can be seen in Worcester's notable bishops all the way back to St. Oswald.

The following two and a half centuries did not as a rule see men of great principle in residence in Hartlebury. The greater number of bishops were either careerists on their way through to better things, such as Thomas Bilson (1596-1597) or Brownlow North (1774-1781) or other careerists whose backing made the relatively well-endowed See with its relatively small jurisdiction a desirable resting place, such as Robert Skinner (1663-1670), James Johnson (1759-74), or the long-lived and querulous John Thornburgh (1616-41). Nonetheless, there are memorable faces in the gallery after John Whitgift; we may do well to glance at three of them.

John Prideaux (1641-50) has left a noble memorial in the diocese, for a remarkable collection, his scholar's working library, now rests in the Cathedral Library at Worcester, as the heart of the Dean and Chapter's collection of printed books. Like Nicolas Heath, he had to stand by his principles under heavy hostile pressure, and like his predecessor, was not found wanting. Not that he appears, any more than the venerable Thomas Morton of Durham, as an ecclesiastical party man of any great strength; Prideaux was much more an Oxford Whitgift, a sober and serious theologian, who had been a solid, thinking centreman in the squabbling Faculty of Divinity, trusted by King James's advisers and made Regius Professor, trusted by his colleagues and elected Rector of Exeter College, trusted by his fellow Heads of House and elected Vice-Chancellor. Late in his life, King Charles I chose him to be Bishop of Worcester when Archbishop Laud's extreme High Church regimen began to break under the assaults of the extreme Calvinists. Both as Vice-Chancellor, and as Bishop, John Prideaux did his best to serve the King while standing squarely by his moderate churchman principles, but it was not a time when moderation could prevail, and the Bishop was ejected from his See and had to live as the pensioner of his daughter's husband, who was left undisturbed as Rector of Bredon in the ejections of 1646-49 until his death in 1650.

Bishop Prideaux was the last bishop for over two centuries who could not be accused of Church careerism. Not until the gentle **Henry Philpott** (1861-1891) left the Master's Lodge of St. Catherine's College, Cambridge with great reluctance to come to Hartlebury, can it be said that Worcester was used by the Crown without an ulterior motive. At times it might be to reward the intrepid defenders of Anglican liberties, such as the forceful William Lloyd (1699-1717) who went on trial as one of the famous Seven Bishops who braved Judge Jeffreys in 1688, or the courtly and kind John Hough (1717-1743), whose staunch stand with the fellows of Magdalen College Oxford against the shameless endeavours of King James II to force upon the College his own disreputable nominee and then, when thwarted, a spineless courtier cleric, has left a shine on his name. Even the royal threat "Elect me the Bishop of Oxford forthwith, or you shall know what it is to feel the weight of a King's hand" failed to cow them. Such men form periods of diocesan good health, for they were not only men of character and duty, but also men of religion who did all they could to rouse their flock. Alas, however, the relative wealth of the See brought to it political nominees, sons of the lesser nobility such as Brownlow North (1774-81) or Ffolliott Cornewall (1808-1831), or such brindled kine as the subject of our last vignette.

Robert Carr (1831-41) as Vicar of Brighton had won the Prince Regent's friendship - a dangerous article as it was to prove, and in due course this was to bring him the Deanery of Hereford and then the Bishopric of Chichester. But it is clear that the price of these preferments had been one beyond Carr's power to pay, for he was already laden with debt when he went to Hereford and even three years with two stipends failed to reduce this debt. His only patron was the dying King, and to George's credit it must be said that he did what he could. The wealthy See of Winchester was snatched by the Prime Minister to assuage the greed of the Sumners, but George managed to secure the reversal of Worcester for his clerical friend and Carr was duly enthroned on 17th December 1831 - just before Lord Grey took his destructive axe to the possessions of the Church of England for the benefits of the Whig landowners as Cromwell had done for the upstart Tudor nobility in the 1530s. All that seems to have happened, however, was that Carr's translation held the creditors at bay a little longer, and in the end the unsecured debts of his profligate Patron caught up with him as he died. Bishops of Worcester had been arrested in their lifetime- Heath is the prime example - but to be arrested for debt in your coffin must be the melancholy sole privilege of Dr. Carr. The noble action of his son-in-law in taking these debts upon himself and spending thirty-five years in poverty trying to pay them off, ensured this otherwise harmless man the dignity of burial. How desperate Carr had been in his endeavours to keep the wolves at bay is perhaps best seen in a remarkable document which his enraged successor Dr. Henry Pepys (1841-60) sent to the Ecclesiastical Commissioners when he arrived to find his one residence, Hartlebury, stripped by Carr of anything that would bring in even petty sums to keep the bailiffs out of the house.

From Pepys onwards, we do not concern ourselves with fur-ther portraits. With the departure of the shameless pluralists (such as Dean George Murray) and the prelates sent to Hartlebury because Worcester was a 'bishopric of ease', and their replacement by men who regarded it as their duty to do more than the minimum in a See where a huge new urban and industrial population had altered everything since Latimer's day, so Worcester, like the other English Sees, rose from slumber and scandal under a different breed of denizens of Hartlebury Castle.

A NOTE ON RICHARD HURD AND THE HURD LIBRARY.
by Graham Cartwright and Mary Parsons.

Richard Hurd (1720-1808) was one of the longer-lived residents of Hartlebury, as well as one of the more learned. He was also the last bishop to add substantially to the Castle building.

Shortly before he was appointed Bishop of Worcester in 1781, Richard Hurd had bought the bulk of the library of Bishop Warburton. His late friend's will had provided that the proceeds from that sale were to go to the Gloucester Infirmary, so that Hurd had the satisfaction of philanthropy too, when he spent some of the money his own literary publications had brought him.

The interest of the library, apart from its beauty of design, is as an example of an eighteenth century scholar's collection. Warburton, himself an eminent scholar (he had annotated Shakespeare's works) had acquired the greater part of the libraries of his friends Alexander Pope and Ralph Allen, after their death, and most of these books had passed, therefore, to Hurd. Many of them contain annotations of their original owners. In 1782 and again in 1805 George III sent the present of a considerable number of books and, of course, there were Hurd's own books, to which he constantly added.

There are, as one would expect, theological works and extensive collections of classical literature. In English literature many of what were then the most modern writers are well represented, as well as the poets and dramatists from medieval times onwards; and the literatures of France and Italy are very fully covered.

Hurd was keenly interested in language, and possessed dictionaries of a remarkable number of languages, both ancient and modern. Books of travel and exploration - in Egypt, Turkey, China, Tibet, to name just a few - are a reminder that as a young man he had published "Dialogues on Foreign Travel". Mathematics, including a number of books on logarithms, science, medicine, philosophy - all these and many more subjects are represented. In their beautiful leather bindings, these books testify to the breadth and depth of Hurd's interests and learning, and, by implication, to the capacious minds of other scholars, nurtured on classical principles in an Age of Reason, and continuing their reading and research well into the Romantic period.

Hurd is more noteworthy for the range of his achievements than for the triumph of one particular talent. He rose from relatively humble beginnings to be a prominent churchman of the period. Though not one of the great divines, he was a respected preacher and defender of the Protestant faith against the challenge of 'Papacy' and 'Natural Religion'. So much so, that he was offered the primacy in 1783, but prudently declined Canterbury as "a charge not suited to his temper and talents". George III, having formerly appointed him to be Preceptor to the two princes, continued to hold him in favourable regard.

On 2nd August 1788, King George III, Queen Charlotte, the Princess Royal, the Princesses Augusta and Elizabeth and the Duke of York, had breakfast in the library at Hartlebury Castle at half past eleven. They were waited on by Hurd himself, whose nephew and namesake wrote an account of the occasion, recalling that Hurd served them "tea, coffee, chocolate, fruit, jellies, etc.".

As a man of letters Hurd edited the works of greater figures, as well as writing imaginative pieces of his own, such as the "Moral and Political Dialogues". Finally, throughout his life he gathered together an impressive array of books which, if it lacks some of the treasures of the true collector, still gained sufficient renown to attract donations from important persons of the time.

Hurd has perhaps been underrated as a critic, although his "Letters on Chivalry and Romance" have begun to receive the attention they deserve, for remarkably heralding the Romantic Age with the pen of an arch Augustan. Dr. Johnson's criticism of Hurd as "one of a set of men who account for everything systematically" does not seem so adverse to a later age, and it is worth remembering that Boswell further records that on another occasion Johnson described Hurd as a man "whose acquaintance is a valuable acquisition". Certainly Macaulay's famous characterisation of the Warburton-Hurd relationship as "Bully to Sneak" does Hurd a measure of injustice, for there is much evidence of Hurd's independent judgement and powers to convert Warburton to a sounder opinion.

It was as a cleric, though, that Richard Hurd chiefly saw himself. Of a retiring nature, he never married, and could seem prim and forbidding to those who only knew him distantly. His views on education, as laid down for the instruction of the young princes, seem strict and severe. Yet Hurd was tolerant by the standards of many around him. While Johnson thought him too much a Whig from his youth, Hurd's friend, the poet William Mason, thought him too much a Tory in his later years. And if he did owe his preferment in part to his naked courting of patronage, he could at least reasonably claim, unlike many of his compeers, that he owed it in part to real merit.

CASTLE AND VILLAGE

A series of essays depicting life at Hartlebury Castle under recent bishops.

Life in Hartlebury in the 1840s.
by Dee Cooper

Bishop Pepys (1841-60)

In 1841 Henry Pepys was consecrated Bishop of Worcester and came to live at Hartlebury Castle, bringing with him his wife Maria and their four children, Henry, Louisa, Herbert and Emily. He seems to have been popular in the diocese, conscientious in the performance of his duties, liberal in his political views, affable and generous to his friends and neighbours, and happy to enjoy the material benefits of his position. That he was an affectionate and understanding father there is no doubt, for we have the evidence of his younger daughter. In 1844, at the age of eleven, Emily took up her pen and, emulating her distant relative Samuel, wrote a delightful journal which gives us a keyhole view of family life at the Castle early in Victoria's reign.

It had been a conscious decision of Henry Pepys to live at Hartlebury for, under the provisions of the 1842 Ecclesiastical Commission, he had the choice of living there or in the apparently much more convenient official residence in Worcester. Hartlebury Castle was large and rambling; the newest parts of the building were at that time more than a hundred years old; it was a dozen miles from Worcester, and it needed an army of servants to run it. But with its large park, gardens, moat and stream, it was an ideal place for bringing up a family.

There is a tendency these days to think that the Victorian child led a dull life, plagued by rigid rules of behaviour and treated too early as a small adult. In Emily Pepys' case nothing could have been further from the truth. With her sister and brothers she was encouraged to take part in games and sports, of which trap-ball and battledore and shuttlecock were favourites. Together they practised archery in Bishop Stillingfleet's avenue of limes and rowed their new boat on the moat, and while Henry went shooting with his friends at Lady Wood and Louisa rode her pony, the two younger children amused themselves constructing a waterfall in the 'River Hartle', as they called the stream running through the park. In summer there were excursions to watch local teams play cricket or to see the Yeomanry parade. Dancing, too, was frequently enjoyed at the homes of friends, and these private balls often continued until well after midnight.

The Bishop's family and their friends were certainly not lacking in energy, and walks, either within the park or as far as Wilden or Bishop's Wood, were a regular activity, while larger excursions 'in a carriage and fly' were made to places further afield, such as Woodbury Hill where they climbed to the top to picnic. It was on one of these occasions that Emily gleefully describes poor Lady Foster battling with stiles, to the delight of her young companions: she 'got over so slow and pulled up her petticoats so high, that there was no end to the things we saw above her knee'. Even 'dear Mama' was not above taking to her heels when caught in a storm on the way home from church: 'Mama got finely blowed, actually having to run all the way from Betty's lodge to the house'. Not the behaviour of a Mrs. Proudie!

A stream of distinguished and titled friends and relatives came to the Castle, and frequent visits were paid by the Bishop and his wife to large houses within a day's drive, but apart from outings with her mother to the local school or to take baby clothes to a poor cottager, Emily appears to have been largely unaware of her humbler neighbours. However, somewhat patronisingly she confides in her diary: 'I do so like going among the poor if they are clean and do not cry as some do'.

The poor at this time unfortunately had quite a lot to cry about, as Emily might well have found had she been older and more aware of events taking place beyond the sheltering confines of the park. The 1830s had been a decade of far-reaching change in rural England. The Enclosures and the Tithe Commutation Act had set fences and hedges around larger holdings of land, leaving in Hartlebury only 200 acres of the Heath as common land and allotting to many parishioners portions of land too small to allow them to make a living. Forced to seek employment, they found that agricultural wages were already depressed, with relief for the poor being a charge on the parish, or in other words the ratepayers. Many agricultural workers whose land holding and wages were insufficient to keep their families were 'thrown on the parish' and whole families were consigned, sine die, to the local workhouse, fathers and sons separated from mothers and daughters, to be dealt with as the Poor Law Guardians decreed. Those workers who flocked into the larger industrial towns to find work in the new factories fared little better. Housing and working conditions were generally appalling, and women and children often worked up to sixteen hours a day to supplement the family income. It is not surprising that throughout

the country there was an atmosphere of unrest and discontent. Among the middle and upper classes a humanitarian concern was growing as they began to be aware of the plight of the working classes in town and country. As the young Queen Victoria came to the throne, reform was in the air; the nation's conscience was awakening.

Hartlebury parish was luckier than most. Poised between rural Worcestershire and the growing industrial area of the West Midlands, its landless population had the choice of agricultural or manufacturing employment, and farmers were forced to pay higher than average wages to compete with local factories. Of course, not everyone was lucky enough to escape the indignities of the workhouse but, writing in the "Statistical and General History of Worcestershire" in 1841, Kenrick Watson was able to give a description of Hartlebury which is far from gloomy. "No parish can produce a more respectable body of yeomanry, labourers better provided for, or poor more kindly treated." The majority of men still worked on the land, but for those who preferred to try their luck in industry there was work at the forges at Titton, the wire mills at Stourport, the quarries which sent sandstone to the ironworks of Monmouthshire and South Wales or the clay pits which provided Titton with its crucibles. A tan yard and a sawmill provided further work, while the new iron and tinplate factory at Wilden employed around fifty men and boys. The servants' halls of the numerous large houses in the area absorbed many local men and girls, and at a nearby spinning mill there was 'work for fifty girls when trade is good'.

The availability of employment in local industry took its toll, however. "Generally speaking" says Watson, "the labouring classes cannot be considered hardy or robust. It would appear that constant communication with a manufacturing district is injurious to their health and habits." It is questionable how much blame should be apportioned to industry and how much to poor housing and inadequate diet. Watson remarks that the children drank hardly any milk and, like their parents, far too much beer and cider; workmen were often paid '9 shillings a week and 3 qts. cider daily' and a consumption of '8, 10 or even 12 qts. a day is very common in harvest.' Overcrowded and damp housing conditions were certainly responsible for much illness, particularly 'consumption' which was rife at that time.

Another major scourge was scarlet fever, which had decimated the parish in 1834/5 and was a constantly recurring danger. Emily describes most poignantly the death of a young mother and her new baby from the disease, caught, according to general opinion, from the doctor who attended her confinement. It is no wonder that the poorer people of the parish had recourse to homely remedies and charms to cure their ailments. Betty Swann, who had a great local reputation as a witch in the 1830s, no doubt did a thriving trade in such charms, one of the least pleasant of which was the

(Left to right): Louisa, Herbert & Emily Pepys from pastel by Catherine Esther Gray 1843

Toad Bag. For this a live toad had its legs broken and was then sewn into a bag and hung around the patient's neck. The family at the Castle, needless to say, did not favour the use of charms to cure their ailments. Ginger tea for a hangover, mustard poultice for a sore throat, a 'nice dose of jalop', or purgative, for general malaise, and calomel and 'a black dose' for lumbago were their homespun remedies.

Hartlebury was more fortunate than many of its neighbouring villages in the field of education. There is evidence that a free grammar school had been founded there in the fifteenth century (p.46) and 400 years later employed a headmaster at a salary of £60 a year and an undermaster. There was also a school for twelve girls, founded in 1728, and several 'dame' schools in which seventy village children received a rudimentary education. The educational experience of the children at the Castle was rather different. Regular morning lessons were an unpopular feature of life for Emily, who describes her routine: "At present I do French exercises for three-quarters of an hour, Maps for one hour, Music, one hour and a quarter, read French and English for three-quarters of an hour, write French copy for half an hour". The fluent writing in her journal attests to her mastery of written English and she read Dickens's newly published books and more improving works for pleasure, but she makes no mention of arithmetic, which was perhaps thought unnecessary for young ladies beyond the mastery of household accounts.

Although industry was beginning to encroach on the area, Hartlebury was still for the most part an agricultural parish. Farms of from 20 to 200 acres were mostly owner-occupied, the majority on a copyhold basis. A handful of freeholders included the Bishop, the Rector and the School Governors; leaseholders paid a rent of 40 shillings an acre on average. By far the greater part of the land was arable, growing barley, wheat and rye, swedes and mangold wurzels for fodder, turnip, peas and beans and vetches which were fed to horses and sold "at a penny a yard". Potatoes were a recent introduction, 150 to 200 acres being given over to their production. Sheep were the major stock, mostly Leicesters crossed with Ross but also some Dorset, grazing in the meadows and under the trees in the cider orchards. Hereford cows were kept, mostly for their milk, and a few pigs, the cottagers' stand-by. Large flocks of turkeys were brought into the area from Wales to be fattened for sale at Stourport market, where the Hartlebury folk could buy 'plenty of excellent vegetables and fruit of every description'. Here butter cost 1s.3d. a pound in the summer, potatoes 1s.6d. to 2s. a bushel, ducks and geese 4s. to 5s. each, turkeys 5s. to 8s. each and fowls 3s. to 4s. a couple. Relating these prices to local incomes, workmen were earning 9s. or 10s. a week and the under-master at the school took home less than £1 a week. At the other end of the social scale, the Rector, the Revd. Thomas Baker, was receiving £2,188 a year, regarded as a very good living, and the Bishop's stipend was £5,000. This latter sum must have been put to very good use, judging from Emily's account of the constant round of entertaining at the Castle, the sojourns at the London house in Grosvenor Place, the concerts and outings, games for the children and visits to the dressmaker.

In comparison to the lively social life led by the inhabitants of the Castle, the villagers of Hartlebury had rather fewer opportunities for revelry. True, there were eight public houses and nine beer houses in the parish, where villagers could enjoy themselves after a hard day's work, but holidays were few and far between. The ceremony of dressing the Maypole took place annually on 29th May, while on the first Sunday after the 25th July, the village held its Wake, a merrymaking to commemorate the dedication of the church; no doubt the autumn brought its share of harvest suppers before winter set in, leading to the then more strictly religious festival of Christmas. It was the church, in fact, which afforded the regular weekly punctuation mark in the life of the Hartlebury villagers and the family at the Castle. It was also their point of contact. Twice every Sunday villagers and Castle folk would attend the recently rebuilt church to hear sermons from the Rector or the Curate and, on Sacrament Sundays and special occasions, from the Bishop himself. During the tedium of the over-long service, Emily would dream of becoming a clergyman's wife and 'doing good to the poor'. Further along the family pew, her mother perhaps planned the next dinner party or, very occasionally, 'went fast asleep, with her mouth open and her head back', while Louisa was probably dreaming of the balls she would attend when she 'came out'; and the poorer villagers filling the pews around them no doubt dreamt of living like the Bishop and his family.

THE FIRST WORLD WAR

A Convalescent Hospital for the wounded was first opened at Woodlands in 1914 and later moved to Hartlebury Castle in June 1915, using as its base the northern stable block which had been converted for use as a College of Clergy by Bishop Yeatman-Biggs. The Misses Frances and Margaret Gibbons were Commandant and Sister respectively of the 8th Voluntary Aid Detachment, Margaret having already seen service on the Western Front and returning to assist her sister in this joint enterprise. Parishioners, including scouts and guides, were encouraged to offer their services. Many entries in Visitors' Books for the years 1915-18 pay tribute to the "great kindness" displayed by the staff and express the gratitude of the patients who, in their own words, "were fortunate enough to be posted to Hartlebury". It also contains many references to Pleck House, the house of the Gibbons sisters which was also used as an annexe for those sufficiently recovered to require little nursing and rehabilitation. With the carnage that was being perpetrated in Europe and elsewhere at the time, it is not surprising that many of the large country houses with spare accommodation were taken over as "Convalescent Homes". That at Wilden, run by the Red Cross with Mrs. Stanley Baldwin as Commandant, was one with which the Hartlebury Home had particularly close relations.

Marked To V.A.D.
Cheer boys it's Hartlebury.

Bottom left:
Margaret Gibbons
Bottom right:
Margaret & Frances Gibbons

Photographs make frequent reference to visits to houses for tea, river trips, boating on local pools, concerts organised by the troops themselves, gymkhanas and garden parties to raise money for the "war effort" in which the soldiers participated. Many of the messages in the Visitors' Book refer to the likelihood of a return "to the front after a short leave at home", accepted without bitterness but with the frequently expressed hope, that, "if I get wounded again they will send me back to Hartlebury". With the conclusion of hostilities and subsequent closure of the unit, many of the effects were sold and villagers were able to join in the purchase of blankets etc.

No similar need for such facilities arose in World War Two, but it is of interest to note that in December 1956 it was not found possible for the offer to the British Red Cross by the Bishop of that day, Mervyn Charles-Edwards, to use Hartlebury Castle as a transit hostel for Hungarian refugees, to be taken up. It seems that this was largely because of the value of the property, its remoteness and the poor prospects of employment which were locally available for the type of refugees likely to be accommodated.

THE END OF AN ERA - 1931-41.

In 1931 a new Bishop, who was no stranger to the parish, came to take up his duties. This was Dr. Arthur Perowne, one time chaplain to his father when he was Bishop of Worcester 1891-1901. He came informally, driving his own car, with Mrs. Perowne alongside, and was welcomed as an old friend, not only by the Vicar and the older inhabitants, but by the school children bearing posies of spring flowers and singing "Home, Sweet Home". He held office for ten years.

His son Leslie writes:

"My first sight of the Castle was on 27th March 1931 when I stayed there the night before my father's enthronement in the Cathedral the following day. But it was not until 1932 that I spent any considerable time living there. The Castle was enormous and all the rooms, even the attics, very big too. A great deal of the house had clearly not been used for many years. Bishop Pearce, my fath-er's predecessor, had been a bachelor, his sister had kept house for him, and much of the furniture, some of it bequeathed to the Castle by Bishop Hurd in the late eighteenth century, had found its way into the wrong rooms and the pictures, apart from the portraits, needed a great deal of attention. We ate in the Great Hall on a beautiful three-leafed mahogany table reputed to have belonged to the great Duke of Wellington. This was family property and with it went six fine Chippendale-period chairs with two carvers, all of which were embroidered by my stepmother, Mabel, and my aunt, Edith Perowne, in an eighteenth century design. I have the chairs yet.

The fine baroque Saloon with its portraits of George I and Queen Charlotte was used only on occasions when visitors were staying. It had two curiosities - one a small cupboard for a chamber pot and the other a Broadwood square piano, the strings of which

Arthur Perowne - *Centreback* as Curate (1893-1901) at Church Guild Meeting outside Rectory. *Centre* - Canon Robertson

were broken and rusty and the action very rickety. It was my ambition to restore it but, alas, I never got round to it and it is still there awaiting the attention of an enthusiast. The room most used by the family was the large drawing room leading out of the Saloon. I never liked it and it has been lost in the recent conversion. One interesting small room built out of what is the present drawing room was the Water Closet, a great novelty.

Apart from diocesan occasions, my stepmother and father did not entertain greatly, but when the Three Choirs Festival was at Worcester, they always invited the soloists and chorus to tea. One year the guests included Bernard Shaw, Mary Jarred and Isobel Baillie. My brother Stewart and I were allowed to have a small house party on some of these occasions. The music was superb and some of the interesting people who stayed at the Castle included Sir Steven Runciman (one of the funniest men I have ever met) and Boris Ord, the organist at King's College, Cambridge, who played two piano duets with Sir Charles Lamb, later to become an Admiral of the Fleet.

Stanley Baldwin and my father were contemporaries. There was an occasion in the thirties when a dowdy looking man appeared

Bishop Arthur Perowne & Mrs. Perowne in Garden

at the front door and asked to see the Bishop. The servant, who told me the story, was on the point of asking him to go to the back door when the Prime Minister gave his name, much to the servant's embarrassment.

My father was a keen gardener and had an ally in the head gardener, Fletcher. In the moat garden were roses and tall yew trees with a fountain in the centre. I christened the end by the moat "Bigg's Bog" after Bishop Yeatman-Biggs who had thought to fill it in to enlarge the garden, but underestimated the amount of infill necessary and the result was a ghastly bog. The gates from the forecourt to the moat garden and the vegetable garden were made from

The Moat Garden

Maltese handwrought bedsteads and, along with a Cedar of Lebanon, now standing in the park south of the moat gardens, were the gift of my brother Stephen, then in Baghdad, on hearing of his father's translation to Worcester.

The Castle was not an easy place to work in; the rooms were all too big but it had great beauty and restfulness and I feel greatly privileged to have lived there."

The Perowne era was the last during which a degree of opulence was apparent in the Castle, for although entertainment was not regarded as extensive*, the house staff included butler, footman, three housemaids and three in the kitchen, together with a head gardener - Fletcher - and two assistants, as well as a chauffeur - Munday. The Bishop, family and personal staff occupied the north wing with guest rooms in the south wing, the centre portion (State Rooms) being used as day rooms. Heating was the problem but was overcome by large coal and log fires. The College house contained a billiard room, much used by the Bishop and his guests.

* An account of a house servant, however, records that in one year they had prepared 2000 meals.

A NEW ERA -

1941-55. *by Joan Cash**

The light was fading on a damp November afternoon as we drove slowly into Hartlebury Village in the ancient family car and stopped to enquire the way to the Castle. We were tired and a little apprehensive and it seemed a long time since we had left London. The house near Biggin Hill aerodrome we had vacated was the only home I had known so it was a major upheaval. A few weeks earlier I had accompanied my father to lunch at the Castle with Bishop and Mrs. Perowne.

"Are we really going to live in the whole place?" I asked my father in dismay. It was all rather overwhelming - though at the same time magical. Mrs. Perowne had been very reassuring, insisting that it was the most homely place on earth.

The great gates of the Castle loomed up in the dusk and from the little pink lodge emerged two rotund figures waving and hurrying to open the gates - Mr. and Mrs. Mantle who were responsible for the 'gates' amongst many other jobs on the estate. In those days people did not work by the clock, rather they fulfilled agreed duties in their own way - perhaps a more creative concept!

The Mantles were both tremendous personalities and delightfully humorous. It was an education to talk with them for there was little they did not know, not only about the Castle and estate, but all facets of rural Worcestershire.

We moved on slowly up the leafless lime avenue. The twin bothies came into view and then the long low line of the Castle beyond the huge circular lawn. The front was lit up despite the blackout and many people were moving about and waving. The resident staff were all staying on and had taken infinite trouble to prepare for our arrival. There were also the head gardener, Mr. Fletcher and the chauffeur, Mr. Munday who lived on the estate. We shook hands all round and hurried inside to find a real feast awaiting us spread out on the huge monks' table. And we slept that night and several nights more in the ancient four-poster beds in the State Rooms. The peace and silence was bliss after the almost permanent state of air raid in London's Blitz, for it was 1941. And the warmth of our welcome made us all feel very much at home.

Hartlebury at that time was a land of plenty, despite the war. Mr. Fletcher was no amateur gardener; in fact he was well-known throughout Worcestershire and much in demand for his gardening lectures. He loved Hartlebury and especially the fine, pink-walled kitchen garden that he had brought to life - now the site of the museum of vehicles, etc. This was always immaculately kept and no space wasted. Two enormous greenhouses sheltered peaches and vines as well as seedlings and cuttings, endless boxes of bedding plants, "experiments" - and several cats to keep down the mouse population! In those days there were virtually no sprays

* Joan Cash, daughter of Dr. William Cash, Bishop of Worcester 1941-1955.

and few insecticides, yet the quality of the produce was first class. Of course there were many insects of all sorts, some of which, thank goodness, much enjoyed the crops of aphids when they appeared! We also kept bees so that apart from having an endless supply of honey, all the necessary pollination was taken care of - a great deal cheaper and more natural than modern methods.

Mr. Mantle was Mr. Fletcher's right-hand man and there were several other toilers in the gardens. Every morning Mr. Fletcher would appear in the kitchen with a basket of samples to find out what the housekeeper required for the day. For my father's birthday in early June he always had plenty of strawberries forced and ready to eat. All year round we wallowed in an abundance of fruit and vegetables of all sorts; peaches, nectarines and figs seemed especially prolific and there was never a shortage of asparagus either. In fact there was such an abundance that every week Mantle would fetch Dolly, a small bay pony; while he harnessed her to a dray, Fletcher would load up the surplus produce - and off they went to market, usually with a local lad dangling his legs from the back and whistling merrily.

Although we had a surfeit of garden produce, meat became very scarce as the war progressed. We found it quite difficult to feed the ordinands who had very healthy appetites and seldom a ration book! And they came for long weekends twice a year in batches of perhaps six or eight. The problem of feeding them was solved when we decided to keep pigs - in one of the garages! Fletcher thought this was a wonderful enterprise for he always enjoyed trying something new. He arranged the somewhat ceremonial pig killings which usually took place at dusk in the stable yard, bringing with him the local slaughterman together with half the village it seemed and there was much noise and jollification. Eventually it was all over and the villagers departed with their trophies - tail, trotters and teeth, etc.! All the ordinands thereafter had pork at every meal and pork sandwiches when they returned from the Cathedral. Fletcher even turned his hand to curing bacon which we consumed all the year round much to my father's delight - he was lost without his bacon and eggs for breakfast.

The Castle was very beautiful at Christmas. In October each year Fletcher lit the fire in the Great Hall and it was not allowed to go out until winter was past and the frosts over. By Christmas it was a blazing furnace and gave out a tremendous heat - so much so that one could not approach too close. We burnt only very big logs from trees on the estate. In those days the walls of the Hall were a darkish red which was exceptionally cosy and pleasant at Christmas. The great fire made a splendid social centre flanked by a huge Christmas tree on one side and a picturesque apple bough complete with living mistletoe on the other - both of course carefully grown and nurtured by Fletcher. Several parties of carol singers would appear with their quaint old lanterns and the odd recorder. They all came in for a drink and mince pies and we then joined them on visits elsewhere. With so many people about and singing the old place really came to life despite the horrors of war in the background.

Domestic arrangements in the Castle were, I must admit, rather awkward from the start. There was the problem of the kitchen which was vast. A solid, immovable oak table took up most of the centre space. There was a temperamental Aga in one corner, the food cupboard in the far distance and the sink across by the back door. And, of course, there were no short cuts across the middle of the room because of the table - it all involved a great deal of footwork! There was no possible place to eat except the centre of the Great Hall and at first we sat on benches at the monks' table. Both table and benches were a good deal higher than an ordinary arrangement - small people's legs dangled which was tiring and you could not move without causing a commotion often involving the disruption of the whole bench! So we returned to our own small table and chairs which looked quite lost and seemed to have an awful lot of space all round. Eventually we altered the spacious but narrow still room which ran behind the Great Hall, between the gallery and the kitchen. It was lined by vast cupboards from floor to ceiling on one side and two large sinks on the other between the long windows overlooking the moat. When all these had been removed it made a very cosy dining room and so much easier to manage. We had beautiful bedrooms and a pretty little sitting room in the wing above the kitchen - all of which is now the very fine County Museum. When we had people visiting we used the enormous drawing room at the far end of the Castle which we furnished ourselves. This room was considerably larger than the Saloon,

which still exists and it took my mother, who had been blind for twenty years, a full ten minutes to reach it from her bedroom at the other end!

Spring was a time of especial beauty at Hartlebury. The first sign was always the appearance of great swathes of tiny Lent lilies on the banks of the moat. Coot and moorhen nested here and their cries echoed across the water as they were perpetually harried by a pair of nesting swans. There were linnets, spotted flycatchers and whitethroats around the bothies, swallows in and out of the stables and always a pied wagtail strutting on the front lawn. The borders around this lawn were beautiful too, blazing with colour; and specially spectacular were the huge oriental poppies in brightest scarlet. There was also a lovely peaceful flower garden in the bed of the moat and here it was warm and very sheltered. One could walk through rose beds and climb to the top of the far side of the moat where was a well-tended grass walk, lined by azalea bushes with ancient mulberry trees at the far end. There was an abundance of wild life all around, both flora and fauna. The undulating parkland beyond the moat and all around contained some

Above
Wedding of daughter of Bishop Cash, Canon Armstrong who officiated on Groom's right, Bishop Cash left of bride, Fletcher and Munday extreme right

Right Portrait of Bishop Cash

lovely old trees and it was grazed by frisky Hereford cattle as well as Dolly, our pony.

In the war years a succession of visitors came, many in need of a peaceful break from the bombs and land mines. We seldom heard a plane, let alone the sound of aerial dog fights and gunfire that we had grown used to in London and it was difficult to believe such a serene oasis could exist in war-torn Britain. The grounds were open to the public every summer in aid of various charities and there seemed to be plenty of clergy meetings and gatherings of all sorts. Life was lived at its slow pre-war tempo. The very elderly Misses Gibbons came to call in their neat little pony and trap and left their visiting cards. These had to be of very particular sizes according to whether one was male or female, single or married - there was a mystique about how many should be left too! It all depended on whether the people you were calling on were in or out; I never could fathom the system but it did not really matter for they were symbolic of a fast vanishing way of life and when the war ended were seldom seen any more. Change was on its way everywhere and that included the Castle.

As the war progressed, Mr. Fletcher's noble bank of outside helpers were picked off for the forces one by one until there were only himself and Mr. Mantle left, both of them too old for military service. Two land girls arrived to help out but it was apparent that the flower gardens had to go and gradually they fell into neglect. The land girls were soon disenchanted with the quiet country atmosphere and indoors the staff were all lured away to the bright lights of Kidderminster and elsewhere. The countryside was now far too slow and dull for the young people. Television was not yet established but was on the way and people were beginning to think in terms of daily entertainment, plenty of dancing and trips to the cinema several times a week. As the forties drew to a close the war was over but rationing remained, rather stricter than ever. Life was very different from the relatively carefree pre-war years of tea parties and indoor games and seldom a background of even the cat's whisker wireless. Domestic staff were rapidly becoming an out-of-date phenomenon. A metamorphosis was occurring and a totally new ethos was being born. Entertaining at the Castle had to be cut to a minimum; there was a certain austerity about and at times it seemed as if we were camping out in an acreage of building for which no use could be found. Frequently there were no more than three people actually sleeping in the Castle, my parents and perhaps a friend or myself or my sister. My mother, being totally blind, had of course never seen the Castle, but coped very courageously - it was difficult. Now life was all rather a worry. I gave up my job and lived at home for two years hoping something more permanent in domestic arrangements might be worked out but I soon began to realise that things were becoming ludicrous.

"No one family can ever again occupy the whole of this place," I thought as I sloshed bucket after bucket of water across the muddied slabs of the Great Hall, "How on earth does one begin to clean it anyway?" And then there was the cooking and shopping and time taken just walking about. It was a depressing prospect but surely there must be some use for this beautiful place, I thought. I remembered the first Christmas we had spent there, the music and the people - always the Castle came alive when there were throngs of people. We used to spend quite a lot of time speculating on its possible future but never quite envisaged what it has now become - which is little short of a miracle in its success.

It all looks much the same outside. Swallows still swoop from the skies, coots still skid across the moat - and the Bishop's family is still in residence. But now there are throngs of people nearly every day - visiting the first class County Museum, or visiting the beautifully kept State Rooms and the Hurd Library; or, best of all, visiting the Great Hall for an evening concert, perhaps a piano recital - this to me is really thrilling. I had no idea the acoustic was so good. The Great Hall is an ideal setting for making music - so much better than its previous role as a dining room. Congratulations to all who were involved in conceiving the alterations which have undoubtedly given the Castle a great new life. Long may it continue to be thronged with many happy people!

1956-1970.*

It had become abundantly clear during the latter years of Bishop Cash's tenure of office that the future of Hartlebury Castle as a home for bishops was being called into question. Two world wars, a depressed economy and changes in the socio-economic climate, meant that the affluence which had hitherto contributed to the standards of luxury being enjoyed by earlier incumbents, usually men of means, no longer applied. The house was too large. The Church Commissioners, although legally responsible for housing the Bishop, had made it quite clear that they were not obliged to finance excess accommodation and that unless a solution could be found to this difficult problem, the whole idea of retaining the building as the See house could be placed in jeopardy. What had once been a house of culture and elegance combined with ecclesiastical dignity, could well be lost to the Diocese after a virtually unbroken history of over a thousand years, during which time it had been the home of a succession of scholarly and at times politically minded divines much exercised in the recurring crises between Church and State.

This was not the first occasion upon which the future of the location of the See house was called into question. Apart from the many houses available at one time to the Bishop throughout the Diocese, there were by 1846 only two official residences: one at Hartlebury and one in Worcester. The need for two houses was

* Based upon documents held in the Muniments Room and written with the assistance of Mrs. Charles-Edwards.

questioned, but the subsequent enquiry came down in favour of Hartlebury and the Palace was purchased for the Dean and Chapter in place of the existing decanal residence, which was to be pulled down.

In 1861 suggestions were made for the selling of Hartlebury Castle and removing the residence of the See back to the Deanery. The Dean and Chapter objected. In 1874, the Mayor, on behalf of the Citizens of Worcester made a similar proposition, but the then Bishop - Henry Philpott - while agreeing that removal to Worcester was desirable, thought that better arrangements could be made. In 1891 Earl Beauchamp offered Hallow Park as an episcopal residence but Bishop Perowne decided against selling Hartlebury. In 1902, Bishop Gore refused to live at Hartlebury, preferring to stay in Worcester, and made proposals for its sale, but local opinion was such that the matter did not proceed, although the Church Commissioners were not unwilling to approve the sale. In 1905, Bishop Yeatman Biggs decided to reside at Hartlebury, subject to certain adjustments to the demesne lands. In 1937 an extensive survey had revealed extensive dilapidations involving the Castle, College, Lodge, detached cottages, boundary walls, gates and fences which necessitated the raising of funds, "to enable certain improvements" to be made.

In 1946 the question of the Bishop being able to afford to continue to live at Hartlebury was raised and a scheme was suggested whereby the Church Commissioners be responsible for dilapidations and certain other costs while letting a large part as a Retreat House or alternatively that the Bishop move to less expensive accommodation. In 1955, a plan for conversion of the south wing into a house for the Bishop, together with a proposal to turn the north wing into "not less than three flats" was put forward, but was not pursued because of difficulties in allocating responsibility for the alterations as well as for the administration of the excess accommodation which, of course, included the Great Hall, Saloon and Hurd Library. On one point all were agreed, that the building was larger than required.

It is possible, therefore, to understand the nature of the problem facing the Church Commissioners with a building much too large for modern needs and with an apparently open-ended and costly maintenance liability. Some alternative plan was certainly necessary and only a successful solution to this problem could justify the continued occupation by the Bishop.

It was in February 1956 that Lewis Mervyn Charles-Edwards was enthroned in Worcester Cathedral and immediately faced with a decision of the Church Commissioners that Hartlebury Castle was no longer suitable as the See house. As a result he had no place in which to live. Following a period in a local hotel, The Elms, at Abberley, he and his wife and family were accommodated in Froxmere Court near Crowle on a "temporary basis" which was to last for nine years. The Bishop was later to describe it as "a

Bishop Charles-Edwards and Mrs. Edwards welcoming guests on the opening of the State Rooms to the public May 13th 1962

Tableau from Extravaganza 1968

delightful place but unsuitable and inaccessible ... which greatly hampered the work of the Bishop".

Bishop Mervyn from the outset, with the strong support of his wife, the Diocesan Conference, Rural Deans and countless others, was determined that he would not be party to any decision to give up the Castle as the See house until he had investigated and assessed the various alternatives which might persuade the Church Commissioners to revise their opinion. So began the lengthy negotiations which were to go on for six years before work was begun to convert the building into the complex as we know it today.

The base lines from which these negotiations were to proceed emerged as follows:

1. That the See house should remain in Hartlebury which was geographically and administratively convenient.

2. Part of the building could be adapted to provide a more modest house and its associated administrative requirements.

3. That other uses should be sought for the remainder even if this meant the limited elimination of some of the inconvenient and less historic parts.

The movement of the See house to another place was never to find favour and there were obvious objections also to the siting of any new house within the precinct of the Castle without prior knowledge of the nature of any future "development" of the main building. Among the suggestions which had earlier been made for this were, a Retreat House, a home for retired clergy, conversion into flats or transference to the Diocesan Authority for use connected with the Diocese.

Other proposals which were made later included the demolition of the north and south wings, leaving the Great Hall and Saloon untouched; the remainder to be remodelled as a house for the Bishops only or that the south wing be converted into a Bishop's House with service flat, and the north wing be demolished or, together with the College, be converted into flats to provide a source of income.

This still left the problem of the future of the State Rooms unsolved. Could it be used for diocesan purposes and what would happen to the Hurd Library for which the Church Commissioners claimed no legal responsibility?

It was not until 1961 that realistic solutions to all the various problems began to emerge when the County Council confirmed their earlier interest in taking over the north wing and adapting it for use as a museum and simultaneously a move was made by interested individuals to establish a Trust to administer the State Rooms for the benefit of the Diocese, making these available for social occasions, meetings, and conferences, as well as opening them up to the public, with the object of helping to pay for the upkeep. This "package", together with the plans already approved in principle to convert the south wing into a Bishop's House with service flat and which would take into account the varying requirements of different kinds of bishops, was strongly supported locally by all shades of opinion anxious to see the Castle restored once more as the base of the Bishop of Worcester.

Many official bodies had been involved in the discussion, which had included not only the Church Commissioners and the Diocese, but also the Ministry of Works, then responsible for Ancient Buildings, The National Trust, the Society for Protection of Ancient Buildings, County, District and Parish Councils and, in addition, many important and influential individuals. Sir Hugh Chance, when Chairman of the County Education Committee, was especially helpful in promoting the concept of a museum.

Early in 1962 the Church Commissioners showed their willingness to support the plan by resolving that tenders be obtained for work on the Bishop's House and the State Rooms, subject to certain financial constraints; that steps be taken to set up a body of Trustees with the necessary resources to take responsibility for the administration and maintenance of the State Rooms; that a lease be negotiated with the County Council for the adaptation and maintenance of the north wing as a museum; that they, the Commissioners, would provide limited funds for the refurbishment of the gardens.

In anticipation of a successful conclusion to these negotiations, plans were drawn up for the opening of the Castle to the public and on Sunday, May 13th 1962, for the first time in 1,000 years (apart from one day when it had been opened in aid of World Refugee Year) this historic event took place. On this opening day various arts and crafts exhibitions were staged and the Band of the 7th Battalion of the Worcestershire Regiment played in the garden to representatives of both county and diocesan life. After the official opening, the Castle was open every Saturday from 12 noon to 6 p.m. and every Sunday and Bank Holiday from 1 to 6 p.m. until Saturday, September 22nd. Volunteers from all the parishes in the Diocese staffed the building with over two hundred individual helpers on Sundays as well as supporters from schools and local organisations. A special guide book was prepared. By the end of the season the Castle had been opened on 40 days and fifteen special occasions had been arranged. Over a thousand helpers had been involved and 7401 visitors were conducted around the building.

In view of the delicate nature of the negotiations taking place at that time regarding the whole future of the Castle, these events could not assume the form of a public fund raising campaign. Nevertheless, the sum of £1,541 was raised towards "the possible restoration of the Castle", but there can be no doubt that if a special appeal for restoration could have been launched, a very large sum of money would have been forthcoming.

By February 1963 tenders had been received, a Trust Deed covering the use of the State Rooms was being drawn up and on the 7th of that month, the go-ahead was given and arrangements made for the furniture and contents of the Library and State Rooms to be stored. The builders moved in on March 4th, hoping to complete the work within twelve months. It was too much to hope that events would progress smoothly and without hitch. Differences between the Church Commissioners and the architect over details were inevitable and caused the Bishop much concern, for although he was in effect only an interested bystander, he had been intimately involved in six years of difficult negotiations and was naturally anxious that the eventual outcome should be successful.

Costs exceeded estimates and a long list of unfinished work was presented in May 1964, but in spite of this, Bishop Mervyn and Mrs. Charles-Edwards moved in to the converted south wing on June 4th and in the words of Mrs. Charles-Edwards to what is now "one of the best See houses in the Church of England" which they were to enjoy for another six years.

It was now necessary to look for ways and means of supplementing the income available to the Trust and amongst the fund raising events to be organised was the Extravaganza of Whit Monday 1968 entitled "Living History". This pageant in gay and colourful costume under the management of Mrs. Charles-Edwards depicted scenes from the Castle's interesting history. Some of the scenes included parts played by past Bishops as hosts to royalty, a setting with Cromwellian soldiers in the Great Hall, Isaac Walton fishing in the moat and a reenactment of the visit to Bishop Hurd of King George III. Many other outdoor attractions provided suitable entertainment for the family. The occasion attracted over 5000 visitors and did much to publicise the venue in its early days. £1,425 was raised, half of which was donated to other charities.

1970 - 1981.

In September 1970, Robin Woods, then Dean of Windsor and Domestic Chaplain to the Queen, was invited to accept the Bishopric of Worcester and was duly enthroned in Worcester Cathedral in March 1971. He arrived having been honoured by Her Majesty with an award of the K.C.V.O. to begin a further period of consolidation and development of the facilities made available at Hartlebury as a result of the conversions completed during the time of Bishop Mervyn Charles-Edwards.

Centrally situated within the Diocese and geographically independent of the Cathedral, Hartlebury Castle proved to be able to fulfil the requirements of providing an excellent and convenient family home with adequate reception rooms, which could be readily supplemented by using the State Rooms - the Saloon as a large drawing room, the Library for staff meetings and small conferences of clergy and the Great Hall for diocesan as well as social, educational and cultural occasions. In the words of Bishop Robin Woods, echoing those of Mrs. Charles-Edwards in 1964, "there is no better equipped Bishop's House in the Kingdom". Other bishops, still saddled with large, albeit historic but inconvenient buildings, now look with envy upon the success of the Hartlebury conversion.

In the 1960s and 1970s, under Bishop Charles-Edwards and Bishop Woods, the grounds and park land were reclaimed and partly replanted. Under the guidance of Henrietta Woods, herself a good gardener and one who kept chickens, ducks, bees and a pony, the garden at the rear of the Castle was slowly brought into care and usefulness. The bank running down to the moat was "terraced" with pathways and shrubs, the old bamboo thicket was made pro-

ductive and the footpath at the side of the water was extended northwards. A footbridge was built over the stream which fed the pool so that a pleasant walk was formed right round the water. External to the original moat and on the mound located to the south of the Castle, the Elizabethans had planted mulberry trees. Two very old trees remain, their lower boughs propped up; the ducks from the moat were seen sharing the fallen fruit each September.

The proposed arboretum was then started but not developed. The plane trees, planted to commemorate Queen Victoria's Coronation, were cleaned up and new trees established in the park to the west of the Castle. With the help of the Local Authority and the Countryside Commission, the main avenue of lime trees was inter-planted to guarantee its future and some new deodar pines fenced in near the village to replace those already two hundred years old and showing signs of decay. The tennis court in the area of the old moat was brought back into action and the new public access to the "wilderness" was made pleasant and welcoming by the Managers of the Museum, the place becoming a picnic area. The old Ice House, carved out of sandstone rock in the eighteenth century, to keep ice frozen in the winter right through into the summer months remains but has become overgrown. Looking south and west from the windows of the Castle, the Abberley Hills were clearly visible, but the encroaching buildings and power lines from Stourport required the planting of new trees, mostly Lawsonia Scots Firs and Wild Cherry on the top of the field beyond the moat.

Thus it was that the Castle itself became well used, by the family of the Bishop in the house, the community of the Diocese and by the general public visiting the County Museum. Also the garden and grounds were put to good use and greatly enjoyed by hundreds of visitors.

Entertainment is, of course, a proper occupation for any Bishop. Hartlebury Castle has proved since its opening in 1964 to be the pleasant and relaxed meeting place not only for the families of successive bishops but also for clergy and laity who come for consultation and refreshment. It was also sufficiently expansive to enable the Bishop over several years to entertain in his own home those who were to be ordained. In the 1970s during June or September, eight or ten men, and later women, stayed at the Castle for their two days of prayer and quiet before going to the Cathedral for their ordination. For the Bishop to become identified with his newly ordained clergy in such a fashion was a real benefit to all concerned.

In addition to his normal diocesan responsibilities, Bishop Woods developed the link, already established, with local industry and in the areas of unemployment which steadily increased in the 1970s. In this respect, the State Rooms of the Castle became the meeting place of many a consultation on social, industrial and educational issues as their leadership faced new and demanding situations. That the Bishop's House should be seen as a rendezvous for gatherings concerned with community issues, including those that affected local government, was seen to be wholly appropriate. In the late 1970s, the Bishop, as Chairman of the Birmingham Board of the Manpower Services Commission, was able to use the Castle as a meeting place for all concerned with employment and new social and industrial demands which were changing the pattern of life, particularly in the Black Country, Halesowen and Kidderminster. Heads of industry, trade unions and government met at Hartlebury with the specific task of creating conditions which would provide for a more socially responsible society.

At the same time the Castle became the ecumenical home for many large gatherings of church workers and Christian organisations in a happy and constructive atmosphere and in so doing also made a major contribution in the field of adult education.

After their years at Windsor, the Bishop and Mrs. Woods were privileged by visits to Hartlebury Castle by several members of the Royal Family. His Royal Highness, the Prince of Wales, came to Hartlebury and occupied the Prince Regent Room on two separate occasions, thereby maintaining the tradition established in the reign of George III. Princess Anne and the Duke of Gloucester were also occasional visitors.

The most notable of the Royal visits however were the day-long visit of the Duke of Edinburgh on 4th May 1978 when, at his own request, he spent a day studying the Diocese at first hand, and the Royal Visit to Worcester on Maundy Thursday 1980 when, accompanied by Prince Philip, Her Majesty the Queen distributed the Royal Maundy at the Cathedral. On the latter occasion, the formal proceedings over, the Queen and the Duke of Edinburgh were guests at Hartlebury Castle, Her Majesty dining in the Great Hall just as her predecessor Queen Elizabeth the First had done in 1575.

The Royal connection greatly facilitated the arrangements for the "Royal Performance" of 11th-26th October 1980. This exhibition mounted to celebrate the 13th Centenary of the Diocese, was devised by Sir Hugh Casson, P.R.A. and portrayed a unique collection of works of art by successive members of the Royal Family over a period of four hundred years. It included works by HRH Prince Philip, HRH the Prince of Wales, Queen Victoria and Prince Albert, together with items graciously lent by Her Majesty the Queen and other members of the Royal Family as well as by museums and private collections. Over 8000 visitors attended and the £7365 raised was devoted to the 13th Centenary Fund set up to encourage and promote the work and mission of the Diocese as an appreciation of our heritage, the Hartlebury Castle State Rooms Trust and the Earl Mountbatten Trust.

Sir Hugh Casson

The change of use of the Castle has added a new dimension to the responsibilities of the Bishops in which their wives can share. Mrs. Louise Charles-Edwards was a tower of strength to her husband in the negotiations and planning for the structural changes and in bringing together a team of "Friends" whose efforts set the pattern for the future use of the State Rooms, while Mrs. Henrietta Woods, who assumed overall responsibility for their administration, was involved in many diocesan occasions and tireless in supervising the ever-increasing numbers of visits and in arranging concerts and exhibitions to bring in the necessary cash for their upkeep as well as building up the reserves of the Trust.

Prince Charles with Bishop Robin Woods, Mrs. Woods and family at Hartlebury Castle

THE PRESENT SITUATION

The See House with its Chapel will continue to provide a comfortable home for bishops and their families in a peaceful environment with the convenience of facilities in the State Rooms for meetings, seminars or conferences associated with their responsibilities as heads of the Diocese of Worcester and now relieved of the burden of caring for a large establishment.

The State Rooms are now administered by a Board of Trustees formally established in February 1966 with its finances in the care of a Trust incorporated in March of the same year. Under the lease prepared by the Church Commissioners, the Trustees are responsible for all repairs and outgoings, subject to a responsibility by the Commissioners for "gross structural failure", a clause which became operative when it was necessary to reroof the rooms completely in 1983. A contribution from the Trustees and major financial assistance from the Historic Buildings Council enabled the Church Commissioners to carry out this costly work and while the property had already been open to the public since 1964, the Council stipulated as a condition of their grant that the Castle be open for at least 30 days a year, to include the afternoons of Sundays and Wednesdays from Easter to September, as well as Bank Holiday weekends and the following Mondays and Tuesdays.

The rooms, which are today available to the public, are the Great Hall, the Saloon, and the Hurd Library, with the Prince's Room open only to booked, guided parties. The Chapel, accessible only via the Bishop's House, is also normally open to visitors on open days. Regular Communion Services are held there on Saints'

Days and major Feast Days at 8.30 a.m. and members of the public are welcome to attend.

The State Rooms are required to be financially self-supporting - apart from the provision for "gross structural failure" referred to above - and to this end have become an established and most suitable venue for a great variety of public functions ranging from exhibitions, concerts, festivals and conferences, to lectures, receptions and money-raising events by charitable organisations. An appropriate scale of charges is laid down, details of which are available from the State Rooms Secretary.

The continuing viability and success of the State Rooms depends upon the energy and enthusiasm of numerous voluntary helpers willing to organise events, act as guides on open days or to carry out the many more mundane tasks behind the scenes. These "Friends of Hartlebury" formalised their concern in 1964 by establishing an organisation with the declared objectives of stimulating interest in, providing finance for and encouraging the use of the State Rooms. They number in 1987 some 150 persons who are invited to an Annual General Meeting and Party in addition to receiving prior notice of the programme of events which is arranged each year. The present annual subscription is £5.00 or £7.00 for a couple. Succeeding bishops have enjoyed the support of many and various committees set up as the occasion demands and are being rewarded by the success of their endeavours in maintaining the fabric of Hartlebury Castle as an important part of our heritage.

The friends of Hartlebury Castle

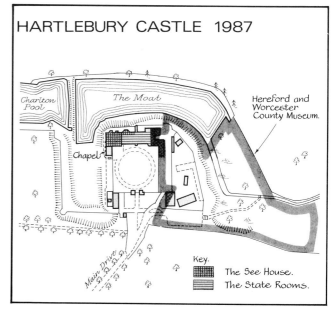

HARTLEBURY CASTLE 1987

Charlton Pool

The Moat

Hereford and Worcester County Museum.

Chapel

Main Drive

Key.

The See House.

The State Rooms.

Victorian Parlour in Museum
(Courtesy of Hereford and Worcester County Museum)

The County Museum which now occupies the North Wing of Hartlebury Castle, was opened in May 1966 to house the collection of the late Mr. and Mrs. J.F. Parker of Tickenhill. Their lifelong interest in history, archaeology and art had resulted in the formation of a Folk Museum in 1937, housed in their historic home in Bewdley. Their collection, largely acquired from large old family houses, reached its climax in the mid 1950s, by which time Mr. Parker had retired from business and was able to devote more time adding to it but also in sharing to an increasing degree its delights with visitors. Before his death in 1962 plans were already emerging for the Collection to be housed at Hartlebury Castle to become the nucleus of a County Museum, under an agreement made between the County Council and his trustees, and when the move actually took place, some thirty tons of museum objects were transferred in addition to a large amount of material which was on loan to other museums.

The original collection has been supplemented and varied to a large extent and new additions are constantly being made. The main subdivisions for display purposes are Archaeology, Applied Art, Domestic Life, Social Life and Trades and Industry. Displays are designed to cover as wide a range of the collection as possible and are changed during each Winter when the Museum is closed to the public.

Financial constraints are delaying plans to take parts of the collection to other sites in the County, but the exhibits both indoors and in the surrounding grounds, are now popular with visitors, especially organised school parties which are admitted free. The Museum, managed by the Education Department of the County Council, is open from March 1st to October 31st daily, except Saturdays and Good Friday.

THE PARISH CHURCH
*by Canon W.H.S Davies**

The first mention of a resident priest, which must be presumed to infer the presence of a church, appears in the Domesday Survey of 1086 and it is further recorded that Bishop Samson 1096-1115 gave "the church of Heartlabiri with the tithes of one hide of land" to the use of the Monks of Worcester as one of his first acts in 1096. Of this church only the lower part of the present font remains.

The church was rebuilt during the thirteenth century and consecrated in 1269 in honour of St. James the Apostle. Of this church the only certain remains are the arches on the north side of the Chancel, the Vestry walls, the east window of which is fifteenth century. In 1567 the Tower was restored by Bishop Sandys 1559-71 and his arms and the date appear on its west side. Entries in the church register which refer specifically to permission granted "to erect a seate right over against the Chancel door" in 1606 would suggest that no seats were provided for the general public at that time. A drawing of the old church shows the entrance to be on the north side near the west end and not through the Tower.

In 1818, Rector Picard restored the "ruinous" Chancel at his own expense and in his will left £1,000 towards the rebuilding of the Nave. Dean Peel of Worcester, who then lived at Waresley House, gave the Porch. His arms are on the west side. The present Nave was built of sandstone from nearby quarries at Chadwick and in Quarry Bank on the old foundation, to plans by Thomas Richman, a Birmingham architect, and consecrated in 1837 by Bishop Carr.

During the period of the rebuilding, the necessary parish meetings were held in the neighbouring White Hart Inn. Between 1877 and 1880 the Chancel was restored internally by Bishop Philpott and at the same time the pews were removed and the present Choir Seats and Reading Desks put in.

The east window of the Chancel was the gift of Miss Isabella Robertson in 1882, the sister of the Rector at that time. It has four lights containing glass by Burlison and Grylls, depicting The Nativity, The Adoration of the Magi, The Baptism, The Last Supper, The Agony, The Crucifixion, The Entombment and The Ascension. The east window of the Side Chapel depicts The Resurrection; this glass is by Clayton and Bell and is a memorial to the daughter of James and Mary Lamb of Waresley. Toward the end of the century the West Gallery under the Tower was removed and in 1908 the ugly painted deal pews replaced by the present seats of English oak. At the end of each of these are carved the names and arms and date of appointment of the Bishops of the Diocese, dating back to 680, a unique distinction for a Parish Church.

* Canon Davies. Curate 1935-37. Rector 1956-74.

The Altar candlesticks were the gift of Bishop Yeatman-Biggs 1904-18. The oak eagle lectern is a memorial to Lady Hampton of Waresley Court who died in 1905, and the Litany Desk to Lord Hampton who died in 1907. The oak panelling around the Altar was originally part of the seventeenth century Bishop's Throne removed from the old church in 1836 and the panelling to the south is a remnant of Norway oak from Peterborough Cathedral, a gift to Bishop J.J.S. Perowne, one time Dean of that Cathedral. The oak altar rails are a recent gift from the Howard family in 1966 in memory of their parents, Mr. and Mrs. Eliot Howard. In 1925 the ornate Bishop's Throne was removed and replaced by one of simpler design in the Chancel near the entrance to the Side Chapel.

Originally the church was ornamented by pinnacles, one of which collapsed in a storm, fell and was destroyed beyond repair. The others, being regarded as equally unsafe, were also removed at the end of the nineteenth century. In 1958 a major programme of repairs and maintenance and redecoration was carried out which included, the renewal of the windows, mullions and glass on the south side of the church, the Vestry and the west end. The eight bells which were rehung at the same time are variously inscribed. The earliest is a pre-Reformation bell, now over 550 years old, and the two most recent were donated by Alfred Baldwin and John Corbett in 1900. The small call bell is dated 1678.

The Church of 1810

The Church of 1269

The Registers date from 1540 with a gap from August 21st 1553 to May 10th 1560. An early extract from the Church Register of 1541 records that Margaret Norton of the age VI score years and two lacking sixteen days was buried XII daie of April. In the early eighteenth century there was a fashion for being married in a place to which neither party belonged. Hartlebury was popular, perhaps because of its association with the Bishop, reaching twenty-five weddings in 1733, eighteen of which were of non-parishioners. Among many interesting burial notes also appear in the Parish Register of 1812, "Body of an unknown sea-faring man found under a hedge together with a purse of eleven guineas. By direction of the Rector and Church Wardens - to the clerk 1 guinea, to the Poor Box 10 guineas". And in 1836, "December 27 Body of an unknown boy found at the sawmill. Buried 1d." In the eighteenth and early nineteenth centuries - great faith was placed in the wearing of rings made from the shillings and sixpences given at church sacrament, for the purpose of keeping away evil spirits or for helping those subject to fits.

The Rectors. The first Rector after the consecration of the church in 1269 was William of Feversham, and apart from a short break during the Civil War, the succession has been continuous - forty-three in number - which gives an average tenure of sixteen years.

His successor was John de Rodberewe. The Chantry of the Blessed Virgin Mary was endowed in 1325 in memory of him and his parents, a small chapel being set aside in the area now occupied by the Vestry. The income provided for prayers for their souls. Such a practice was common up to the time of the Reformation when Henry VIII sequestered many such endowments. In this case they were transferred to the Grammar School.

A murder in the church in 1375 caused great problems. The perpetrator of this foul deed was excommunicated, the church closed and parishioners only permitted to use neighbouring churches until the church was "reconciled". This included the payment of a fine. Payment was delayed as a result of which neighbouring clergy were instructed to "warn all Hartlebury folk to be good". This was sufficient to ensure that the money was paid and the church "reconciled" on 17th August of the same year.

The first Rector to become a Bishop was Adam de Moleyns, Bishop of Chichester 1433, later assassinated at Portsmouth when preparing to sail to the Continent, having become unpopular after his share in the introduction of Margaret of Anjou as bride for Henry VI. Thomas Garrett 1538-40 was burned at the stake by Henry VIII, one of the earlier Protestant martyrs. Rector Miles Smith and Bishop Bilson both lived at Hartlebury at the same time and assisted in the revision of the Bible published in 1611 - Miles Smith later becoming Bishop of Gloucester. His successor, John Lesly, became Bishop of the Isles, Scotland.

One of the most illustrious of the long line of Rectors was Richard Bentley 1695-98, a celebrated Classics scholar, later to become Master of Trinity College, Cambridge. He was succeeded by James Stillingfleet, a son of the Bishop, at the age of 24, and became Dean of Worcester in 1726 but continued his association with the parish by retaining the living until 1737. It is to him that we owe the present Rectory, built for him in 1700, and during his time the church bells were recast (five only at this time). He was succeeded by his son who lived on as Rector for forty-two years - a total of eighty-one years between them. Five Bishops of Worcester are buried in the churchyard: Bishop Hurd 1781-1808, Bishop Carr 1831-41, Bishop Pepys 1841-61 and Bishops J.J.S. Perowne 1891-1901 and Arthur Perowne 1931-41, the former's son.

There can be little doubt that the desirability of a close liaison between the Rector and the Bishop of Worcester influenced the selection of incumbents and would account for the generally high calibre of those nominated for this desirable appointment, which for many years boasted of the assistance of two curates and which enabled the Rector to hold other preferments and to absent himself should he wish to travel. Relations between Bishop and Rector were not always friendly. A Bishop's son, out shooting one day, peppered the gamekeeper in the leg and walking up to apologise said, "I'm awfully sorry, I thought it was the Rector".

By contrast an austere and unfriendly bishop gave a cool reception to a visiting parson who wrote the following lines and attached them to the entrance to the drive:

A Castle without any cheer
A Cellar without any beer
A Park without any deer
The Bishop of Worcester lives here

Nepotism is therefore reflected in many examples of appointments. In 1623 Bishop Thornborough incurred the displeasure of the King by appointing his son-in-law, Emmanuel Smythe, at a time when he - the King - had in mind to offer the living to Dr. John Lesly. The Bishop's excuses were regarded as "not sufficient", Smythe resigned and Dr. Lesly was duly appointed. When, in 1624 Lesly became Bishop of the Isles in Scotland, Thornborough had the satisfaction of reappointing his son-in-law, who served as Rector from 1625-70 with a break during the Commonwealth. He was followed by William Skinner, the son of Bishop Skinner, who served till 1695 to be replaced by Richard Bentley, who filled the vacancy for three years before becoming Master of Trinity College, Cambridge. In 1698, James, the youngest son of Bishop Stillingfleet, was appointed and in due course his son, Edward, carried on the tradition, holding the living from 1737 to 1777. The next Rector, 1777-1801 was a nephew of Bishop North and his successor 1801-1818 was Richard Kinvert, a cousin of Bishop Hurd. He held four other livings in addition to Hartlebury, namely Knightwick, Hallow, Grimley and Alvechurch and it was well that he had other curates to help him. Samuel Picart, who succeeded, was no relation but was followed in 1835 by Thomas Baker, a son-in-law of Bishop Carr, who served till 1877, only to be succeeded by John Haveland, a brother-in-law of Bishop Philpott. He was Rector until 1880 when the long period of nepotism in Hartlebury ended. There was little hope for the preferment of the poorer clergy under these circumstances.

Other places of worship. The Mission Church of St. Mary's at Bishop's Wood was built by Bishop Henry Philpott in 1882. He died in 1891, a much-loved Bishop, and chose to be buried there. The Lychgate was later erected as a memorial to him. It is now only used as a cemetery chapel.

The Chapel of St. John's at Summerfield started as a church room and men's club in 1895 to meet the needs of a growing population in this area. It was consecrated as a church in 1916. Being constructed largely of corrugated galvanised sheeting, it soon acquired the title of the "Tin Tabernacle", by which name it is still referred to with affection.

A Congregational Chapel at Crossway Green was erected in 1870 and serviced by ministers from Kidderminster. It was demolished along with other buildings during the course of road widening in 1936.

The Church after restoration

interior

The Church today

SCHOOLS

The Village School
by Edgar Sobey

The pattern of education in Hartlebury was very similar to that of other places. There was probably an ancient school, founded by a generous benefactor of an earlier age, for the sons of the local gentry and farmers, but for the ordinary village boy or girl there was little or nothing available. Occasionally the curate instructed the children in scriptural matters, teaching them to read, write and do simple arithmetic. These efforts, however, were haphazard and spasmodic and it is notable that no provision was made for the teaching of girls; domestic skills were thought to be enough.

In the early nineteenth century, however, little local schools began to appear, so-called "Dame Schools" where for a small weekly fee, an elderly woman taught children in her kitchen, reading, writing and, above all, the Catechism, while she continued with her domestic duties. All this was changed when the Education Act of 1870 made school attendance compulsory and free for all children up to the age of thirteen. Committees were set up to implement the provisions of the Act. One of these committees was set up in Hartlebury in 1876 under the chairmanship of the Rector, the Revd. John Haviland. Applications for Grants were made to the Church Society, the Charity Commissioners, and other local bodies, while a Public Subscription list was opened. By the end of the year more than £7,000 had been raised and the Rector gave part of his orchard for a site on perpetual loan with the proviso that, should the building ever cease to be a school, the land would revert to the Rectory.

After much discussion and examination of plans, these were agreed and the contract to build was given to James Cook, a local builder, whose monogram in stone is set in the south wall of the building. Basically, it was one long room divided into two parts, the larger portion being twice the size of the smaller. The smaller room with a "stepped" gallery was for the infants, and the larger room for the rest of the children could be divided by a sliding partition forming two classrooms. It was heated by two large fireplaces and two "Tortoise" coke burning stoves and lit by four large oil-burning lamps. The children sat at long pitch-pine desks on benches with no back-rests, and in many cases their feet were off the floor, a most tiring and unhealthy position. The only water supply was a pump in the playground, and sanitary arrangements were primitive. The whole area was fenced in with spiked iron railings and separate play areas for boys, girls and infants were strictly maintained.

The school was opened on Monday, 14th October 1878 with Mr. George Austin as Headmaster and his wife, Mrs. Austin, in charge of the infants. Eighty-six children were admitted on the

Gardening and cookery classes in early 20th century

opening day and by the end of the month numbers had risen to 135, many of whom it is recorded were totally illiterate.

An examination of the Records shows a steady application to work, detailed examination of classes and subjects, reports by Inspectors, both Diocesan and Government, and an increase in numbers. In common with all rural schools, children were frequently absent doing farm work, pea-picking, fruit picking, potato picking, going to the hop-yards in the Teme Valley and Hereford, casual work on the land forming a large part in the family calendar and economy. "February 1889 extremely hard weather, deep snow, roads impassable." "1896 school closed for six weeks due to an outbreak of fever" (diphtheria? scarlet fever?).

Mr. Austin retired in 1892 and was succeeded by Mr. John Cox who remained until 1923. During the thirty years the school was under his control, it earned for itself the reputation of, "....standing high among the best in the County of Worcestershire". Mr. Cox was a man of strong personality, dedicated to his profession and yet "if severe in aught, the love he bore to learning was at fault". Under his guidance, the school flourished, numbers rose to over 220 children, an extra classroom was built in 1912, music and rural

The School Today

sciences were introduced, while the standards of discipline and achievement consistently received high praise from the Inspectors. In 1923 Mr. Cox retired to live in the village he had served so well. He died in 1953 in his ninetieth year, a greatly respected figure whose reputation and personality are still spoken of to this day.

He was succeeded by Mr. Ernest Langford, a quiet scholarly man who unfortunately did not enjoy very good health and was frequently absent from school. However, he maintained the high reputation of the school and did much to foster the close relationship between the Church and the school. He retired in 1940. His successor, Mr. Norman Cox, was a notable musician and was planning to extend and develop music in the school when he developed a fatal illness. He died in 1943 and was succeeded by Mr. Edgar Sobey who now lives in Stourport after twenty-five years as Headmaster. It was during his time that education of the County children was broadened by making greater use and appreciation of the environment in which they lived. In 1953 he produced a Coronation pageant held at the Castle and in Bishop Charles-Edwards's time arranged for Christmas concerts which were held in the State Rooms.

Hartlebury Church of England First School is a place that has always had an enviable reputation for happiness, dedication and performance, encouraged no doubt by the fact that only seven headmasters have served the school in its 107 years' existence.

Numbers attending today are much reduced to just over seventy. This is the result of a combination of factors affecting many country schools: a declining birth rate, a reduction in the age range catered for, as well as a tendency for the more affluent society to use facilities provided in the private sector. "Leavers" at the age of eleven continue their education at Burlish Middle School in Stourport.

The Queen Elizabeth Grammar School.
by Mary Parsons based on a manuscript by Dr. D.A. Guyatt.

There is some evidence that the precedessor of this school existed in Hartlebury even as early as 1472 and in 1501, when a newly appointed Rector was described as, "magister, clericus, preceptor" (master of arts, clerk and teacher) some degree of formal instruction must have existed. By 1556 there was certainly an established school in the village, known as "the free school at Hartlebury" and financed by rents for lands originally belonging to the Chantry of the Blessed Virgin Mary (established in 1325) in St. James's Church. When these lands passed to the school, when the first schoolhouse was built and the first master appointed, remain unanswered questions, but the Order Book of the Trustees who administered the properties records in 1556, "The schoolmaster this year had the schoolhouse and the close garden adjoining to his own use".

Two years later, the first year of Elizabeth I's reign, Bishop Sandys secured for the school a royal charter. "The Free Grammar School of Queen Elizabeth in Hartlebury", as it was now to be called, was to have a master and usher and twenty governors from the parish, with power to appoint and dismiss the masters and to make statutes of government for the school. With the help of the Bishop, these statutes were finally produced in 1565, and stated that the masters were to "teach virtue and good learning, and the true knowledge of God and His Holy Word, and one afternoon in every week, teach the scholars to write and cast accounts".

Meanwhile, the masters would have the profits of "all such cockfights and potations as be commonly used in schools". One suspects that these activities were more to the taste of some pupils than the afternoons of writing and casting accounts for, two generations later, in 1616 the Order Book recorded "the building of a Brewhouse and Chamber and Cockloft over it, for Mr. Pierce our head schoolmaster".

The schoolhouse built, of course, on charity land, was a timber-framed building, fifty feet long by eighteen feet wide, standing in front of the church, and with the master's house adjacent. The churchyard and drive served as the boys' playground. In 1596 the schoolhouse had glass put in the windows and from then on glaziers' bills are a regular feature of the accounts until in 1713 a glazier was placed on a yearly contract. The boys, it seems (or should outsiders be blamed?), regularly broke not only the windows but the lock and key, installed in 1604 and during the next century repaired or replaced every five years or so. Inside were a main room where the usher most likely taught the younger children to read, write and count, and an inner chamber used probably by the schoolmaster for teaching the Latin and Greek implied by the school's title of "Grammar School".

The Gables

An inventory of 1585 records a brass pot with a link, a pair of andirons, two pieces of pewter, one table in the hall, three forms and six benches and one press (i.e. cupboard) for the inner chamber. Gradually during the seventeenth century, blackboards were introduced, but it is not until 1694 that there is any mention of books and then only for the cost of the chains which secured them - clearly a necessary security measure in a building with broken windows and forced locks. In 1695 the single chain needed to anchor the dictionary cost one shilling and twopence.

In 1702 the by now dilapidated schoolmaster's house was replaced by the house called The Gables, still standing. There was also an usher's house in Quarry Bank, for there is a record of the repairs carried out on it in 1724. Towards the end of the eighteenth century, it was decided to build a new school house, up the road off Quarry Bank, skirting the usher's garden. In 1794, therefore, the boys moved to a new and more convenient building, with a playground adjoining, which was the schoolhouse until 1912. In that year, much larger premises were built farther up the hill, but the old building was still in use as a diningroom and artroom. The 1912 buildings, with extensions, were the Grammar School's final home, for the County's change to comprehensive education in the 1970s meant that boys and girls from the Grammar Schools in the area attended a school on the site of the Kidderminster Girls' High School.

How troubled Bishop Hurd would have been could he have foreseen these days of co-education. In 1798, whilst he was Bishop, the School Governors made an order to grant a lease of the old school building to someone intending to erect a Girls' Boarding School. The Bishop used his influence to see that instead the old building was taken down and the site used to enlarge the churchyard, for, he declared, "As the premises are almost contiguous to the house in the churchyard belonging to the Headmaster,......I objected to their being applied to such a purpose (i.e. a Girls' Boarding School) which I thought would be injurious to a school for boys".

The Governors of nearly a century earlier had been in more serious trouble with their Bishop, the scholarly Bishop Lloyd. He clearly mistrusted their judgment in appointing a schoolmaster and their efficiency in keeping accounts, and wrote in 1705 to castigate them for their laxity. After stating that the salaries they were paying were insufficient to attract able teachers, and advising caution in the renewal of leases in order to raise their income, he then continues, "As a new headmaster is soon to be appointed, I would advise you to lay aside all your private interests and piques, and to agree together to choose the best man that you can find". He also reproves them for using school money for their own wining and dining - quite unnecessary, "since you all live within the Parish, where you have meat and drink at your own houses". They should hold their meetings in the church or the schoolhouse, "where it

may be done much better than at an alehouse. There especially is the worst place for making up of your accounts: though I am afraid you make them all there, for I cannot imagine how they should be done so slatterly otherwise". Within the next few years all but one of these unsatisfactory Governors must have either died or been disqualified and, as the Bishop was approaching the age of ninety, he seems to have been content to leave the Rector, James Stillingfleet, son of his own predecessor in the bishopric, to act alone when making a new appointment of Headmaster. In 1716, Stillingfleet wrote in the Minutes, "I being ye sole Governor of the Free Grammar School of Hartlebury ....do hereby elect, nominate and appoint the Revd. Mr. William Boughton, late schoolmaster of Chaddesley, to be Headmaster of the said Free Grammar School".

Clearly, during the next two and a half centuries the Governing Body, like all organisations, reflected the temper and attitudes of its own small community and, to some extent, of English society as a whole. The only Chairman widely known outside his own county was a twentieth century one, Earl Baldwin of Bewdley, and one likes to hope that the Speech Days he attended in the 1940s were of genuine interest to this considerable scholar and lover of Worcestershire, and that he found much to commend. The gates still at the entrance to the school are a reminder of his long service. The inscription on the pillar alongside reads, "These gates were presented to the First Earl Baldwin K.G. by the Worcestershire Association and first set up at Astley Hall. They were presented to the school by the second Earl in 1953 to mark his father's long

Bowbrook School

tenure of chairmanship of the Governing Body".

Of the boys and masters who worked together in this school community we know little for certain beyond the names, of course, of the Headmasters and Ushers and the fact that the Headmaster was frequently, though not always, the Curate of the church. The original schoolhouse could not have accommodated more than thirty boys, which seems in fact to have been the maximum number, certainly up to 1798. At first the school was literally "free" for all pupils, until in 1672 one William Skinner, a Governor and Rector of Hartlebury, wrote, "The Governors have agreed that no other children but such whose parents are parishioners and inhabitants of this parish of Hartlebury shall have the benefit of being taught free without paying the schoolmaster for their teaching."

Much later in 1807, we find a Hartlebury resident writing to ask Bishop Hurd about two brothers at the school, named Baldwin: "they were taught free", he writes, "in the time of Mr. Harward, but since the new master has been at school he charges one shilling and sixpence per week for each of the two boys. Have the boys a right to be educated free or not? Baldwin lives at Tin-mills in this parish."

How this was resolved is unknown. When a new Headmaster, the Revd. John Harward, was appointed in 1808, he began to take private, fee-paying pupils, some of whom boarded in The Gables, which was considerably extended for the purpose. The top floor was used for dormitories, and names and dates of boarders can be seen carved in the floorboards and scratched on the leads outside the windows.

Mr. Harward ceased to take boarders about 1825, but the undermaster received some for a few more years. After 1832, however, he had no fee-paying pupils, but taught reading, writing and accounts to all the Hartlebury children whose parents wanted to send them. In some respects matters had changed little since Bishop Lloyd's letter a hundred years earlier. Governors were still frequently the school's tenants, rents consequently undervalued and salaries iniquitously low. By 1814, John Harward's salary at £36.00 was only £4.00 more than in Lloyd's day (1699-1717), whilst the undermaster's had risen in the same period from £12.00 to £18.00, so that one sees why they wished to supplement their incomes with boarders' fees. So strongly did they protest at their niggardly pay that their salaries were raised to £60 and £40 a year. Still dissatisfied, however, the masters consulted a lawyer and were advised to go to the Court of Chancery. After a visit to the school in 1832 from the Chantry Commissioners, the Attorney-General finally filed a bill in Chancery and the school was closed in 1841.

Eleven years later it was reopened but with a number of changes in its constitution. Governors could be chosen from those living within ten miles of the parish; boys learning only Latin and Greek would pay nothing; other learning would cost up to two shillings a week; the Headmaster could take fifteen boarders, the undermaster eight; their salaries were respectively £200 and £100, and they lived rent-free. Meanwhile £500 had been spent on repairs to their houses, and when the new Headmaster, the Revd. Edward Firmstone, took up his appointment, he had ten free boys and seven boarders under him, while the second master, Mr. G.E. Tarlton, from the City of London School, had charge of thirty-two free boys.

All did not run smoothly, however. There were complaints that the Headmaster did not share the teaching of his scholars with

Mr. Tarlton, and that he dismissed them ten minutes earlier than the others every day. It was further objected that the free boys had two half holidays a week instead of one, and that bad language of these "lower class boys" was injurious to the school - though it was added that "the working were not the only classes that used bad language".

If the number of shortcomings appearing so far in this account seems disproportionate, this is because they were more often recorded than the successes. When faults were brought to light, it was surely because of a genuine concern among the parishioners of Hartlebury. for the highest possible standards in the school they respected and valued. During more than four centuries, the masters and boys who studied - and played - together must have shared much sound scholarship in that small and closely-knit community. Certainly this was so in the School's last decades, when about a hundred and twenty boys, many from outside the parish, received a good academic education and attained a creditable number of university places. Their prowess in hockey led several of them to the Schools' Olympics, and in soccer and cricket too, their performance frequently excelled that of much bigger schools. No doubt much of this was due to the influence of R.E. McKinley who not only attended the school as a pupil but who returned to spend his entire teaching career there. He displayed outstanding versatility in all ball games, coaching the boys in cricket, football and hockey, taking up golf when he could no longer represent Worcester at hockey at the age of seventy-four. A legendary figure indeed who died only three years ago.

Mr. Pearman, who became its Head for the last year or two before it closed, recalls his time there with affection. He remembers the morning they turned up to find part of the school burnt down and the big bell molten and vanished. It was a matter of pride that the school did not close for a single day, as some classes were accommodated at the Castle. He speaks of the school's good discipline, of the boys' pleasing appearance in their distinctive maroon blazers and he is happy to describe the way the school spent its very last day in July 1977. On that day the School Fund was put to its final use, that of financing a splendid party for every member of this, the first school in England to be called "The Queen Elizabeth Grammar School".

In September 1977, "Bowbrook", a private school, moved in to occupy the site. This co-educational, non-denominational school takes children from three years old up to GCSE level and in addition to the original site of eight acres in Quarry Lane has acquired a further six acres and buildings a mile away in what was the Officers' Mess of the R.A.F. Maintenance Unit. This "Little Bowbrook" houses children up to seven years of age. The school today caters for some two hundred pupils and attracts children from a wide area, encouraged by the provision of coach transport. The games facilities are willingly made available to local clubs.

THE CHANGING FACE OF HARTLEBURY

"We walk every day among witnesses of history who probably never talk about it."

Much of this section of the narrative will be devoted to an account of those changes which have affected the parish within the present century. It is based upon the recollections of individuals who have been kind enough to share them with the editor, supplemented by information gleaned from records held by the County Record Office and Libraries. Although this account of recent historical material is of necessity superficial, it is hoped that the range selected is wide enough to interest present generations and even to encourage others to make further use of the wealth of information which exists and which official sources are only too willing to make available to anyone interested in Local History.

A proportion of the text is also based upon manuscripts submitted by individuals and these sources will be acknowledged as the story unfolds but the editor accepts full responsibility for the compilation into a continuous narrative.

Extensive reference has already been made to the strategic importance of Hartlebury Castle during many centuries when much depended upon the relations between Church and the State but it should not be forgotten in this age of motorised transport that present highways are largely based upon early roads and tracks and that it was only in 1888 that the responsibility for the upkeep of main roads was taken over by County Councils and that of other parochial roads by District Councils in 1894.

It must be of interest, therefore, to relate the origins of those early highways, concerned primarily with traffic between early settlements, to the present day. In this respect we are fortunate that one* who was closely involved in much of the development of major roadworks in the district lived within the parish for many years, spent many hours walking the local lanes and applied his professional knowledge to provide the information upon which the following account is based.

For many centuries the movement of populations and their goods depended upon rivers and tracks established by common usage. The River Severn, navigable in all seasons until about 120 years ago from the Bristol Channel to Pool Quay near Welshpool, a distance of 155 miles, was one of the main arteries serving the Midlands, and tracks were determined by the ease with which it could be forded. Used by the Romans for trading purposes, it was confirmed by an Act of Parliament in 1430 as "The King's Highway of Severn". Some fords were little better than stepping stones, while others could provide passage for horse drawn vehicles or droves of

* R. Frost

animals, all of course made difficult at times of flooding to which the Severn is especially prone.

One of these main crossing places bringing traffic from the west was at Redstone Rock, leading to Sandy Lane on the east. This would naturally lead to the establishment of a track to the Castle via what are now Barracks Lane, Mill Lane and Hillditch Lane. Other tracks later branched from this in the Titton area; one to Droitwich, the centre for the distribution of salt - a very important commodity in those days - which proceeded via Crossway Green, Stoney Lane and Elmley Lovett; one towards the West Midlands via Hillditch Lane, bearing left to Lower Poolands Farm - now called Hillditch Farm - across the common land by Wilden Top, Summerfield and Stanklyn Lane; one which left Sandy Lane to go across the lower part of the Common via what is now Kylemilne Way in Stourport, Wilden Lane, Chester Road South and north towards the north Midlands.

A further early track dates back to the time before a cutting was made through rocks adjacent to the Castle. This diverted from Hillditch Lane via Charlton Lane and Torton Lane, across what is now the Droitwich-Kidderminster road, through a narrow rock cutting which can still be seen and on again to the West Midlands, thus in part at least preceding the A450. As the population increased and more of the forests were cleared, a further network of highways developed as narrow winding lanes, used mostly by packhorses but unsuitable for wheeled vehicles other than farm carts.

Until the eighteenth century the work and expense of maintaining these highways were levied upon the inhabitants of parishes through which they passed. These duties were enforced by Common Law with responsibility vested in local authorities. At the end of the seventeenth century a parish rate could be raised to provide hired labour in place of that which was previously "voluntary" and unpaid.

Privately vested Turnpike Trusts, which were authorised to recoup these expenses by the levying of tolls upon road users, were legalised in 1663 and during the following two centuries hundreds of such enterprises grew up and many new roads were established. Two Turnpike roads in Hartlebury can still be identified, one from Kidderminster to Worcester, the original A449, and a second from Stourport to Crossway Green, the A4025. The former passed through the village via Rectory Lane and Quarry Bank. It was not diverted past the Talbot Inn until much later, at which time the width was only sixteen feet between cottages opposite the Post Office and a butcher's shop, barely enough for two vehicles to pass. The precursor of the A4025 ran across the Common where it is relatively straight and later necessitated a cutting being made through the rock at Titton, work said to have been done by prisoners of war during the Napoleonic Campaign. The earlier track here went round the front of Oakley, across the present line of the road and so on across Lincomb Lane.

Tollhouses for the collection of charges have only recently been demolished at Mountbank and at Goldness Corner. Others are recorded at the Mitre Oak, Bugle Gate and by the Old Anchor Inn - Mitton Gate - but doubtless there were many more.

Road development was also affected by various enclosure awards of the nineteenth century. Such roads across common land were relatively straight, as can be seen in those sections which run along Wilden Top to Summerfield and Stanklyn; from the Mare and Colt towards Kidderminster and in Bishop's Wood Lane.

The advent of canals in the eighteenth century and railways in the early nineteenth century resulted for a time in a widespread decline in the use of roads for heavy traffic. The introduction, however, of macadam surfaces in the early nineteenth century - stone chippings of various sizes spread and rolled in layers bonded with soil and water - and the use of tar and pitch as a bonding agent later in 1883, again revolutionised road transport by providing a surface upon which, first solid rubber tyres and later inflated tyres could be used.

The tale is told and it could well be true, of two ladies earlier in this century out for their afternoon walk and approaching each other from opposite directions. Crossing over to pass the time of day, one remarked, "I thought it was you, you thought it was me and now we find it was neither of us". The significance of this anecdote lies in the fact that it is not long ago that everyone in a parish knew everyone else and individuals were identified by their particular occupation, their role in the community or even by their eccentricities.

Many factors have contributed to this change. Changes in farming practice have greatly reduced the numbers dependent upon it for their livelihood and have largely destroyed the intimate inter-family relationships which it engendered; the younger generation no longer find employment locally available; the availability of modern methods of transport attracts urban dwellers to enjoy the pleasures of the country and many take advantage of the depopulation by the indigenous population to take over and modernise accommodation which becomes available. In addition, of course, the general increase in the standard of living has encouraged a more mobile population to wish to share the undoubted pleasure of "living in the country" and many villages find themselves included in the strategic plans of District Councils for housing development to meet this demand, Hartlebury is no exception.

Rural communities were for many centuries largely self-contained and able to meet their everyday needs locally except for an occasional day out in the nearest town or with the help of the

Construction of bypass

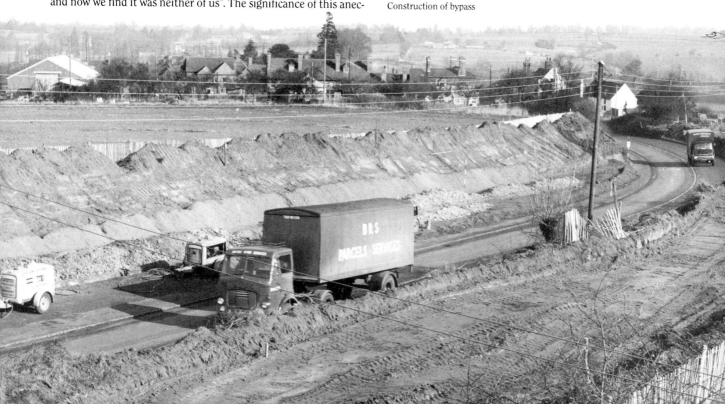

few more affluent or more mobile such as farmers who would willingly add a few errands for friends to their own shopping list. Regional directories such as "Kellys", which became available in the early part of the nineteenth century, help to underline the point, and the year 1881 provides an appropriate starting point for this comparison. At that time in the Parish of Hartlebury there were ten public houses, many cottages with a room set aside for the sale of home brewed ale or cider, four general stores, butchers, bakers and grocers, two blacksmiths, three building contractors, two millers and, in addition, individual craftsmen such as carpenters, wheelwrights, plumbers, engineers, tanners and shoemakers. The women folk also played their part in supplementing the meagre wages of the men, the unmarried "going into service" and the others taking in washing, sewing and mending and "outwork" for cottage industries or, once the family was grown up, returning to "service" on a daily basis. Even in 1930 a similar spread of services remained with the significant addition of three garages, one motor haulier, a brickyard and even a sub-branch of the Midland Bank! This was indeed a time when "everone knew everybody".

Social changes were greatly accelerated by the Second World War which introduced into the parish two major industrial concerns, the R.A.F. Maintenance Unit (1938) and a Small Arms Factory (1940). The agricultural industry was also faced with a challenge to provide an increased volume of home-produced food. Even the railway station also suddenly became more important in order to meet the demands from passengers coming in to work and from industry seeking an outlet for its products. A staff of stationmaster, foreman, signalman, two porters and two clerks was necessary. Today, the two industrial centres remain, albeit with different purposes, to add to the revitalised Brickworks as important sources of employment but farms are highly mechanised and employ only a small fraction of their earlier workforce. The increasing use of road transport has reduced the station to an unmanned halt, and the majority of local services and small industries have gone. Two post offices, three village stores remain and boundary changes of 1933 transferred a considerable percentage of the population to Stourport. The parish now has five public houses, but no ale or cider cottages.

Thus, from being self-sufficient, the parish has within the passage of fifty years become mainly dependent upon adjacent urban centres for services and employment and has changed in character to become a popular dormitory for a commuting public. It is more fortunate than many in that it has retained its schools, has a fine Village Hall as a centre for a multiplicity of social occasions and, although the church now shares its incumbent with neighbouring parishes, it retains the presence of the See House for the Diocese of Worcester at Hartlebury Castle as a constant reminder of the important part which its presence has played and will continue to play in the life of the community.

While older generations retain nostalgic memories of the "Good Old Days" - good for some and accepted by those who knew no other - and regret the break-up of family ties which bound the people together, no one would wish to turn the clock back. Newcomers therefore have a responsibility to understand and appreciate the background to those changes which have taken place and to support the "natives" in any measures designed to preserve the best of the past upon which the present is surely founded.

AGRICULTURE

This is and will remain the largest and most important rural industry. Most of the available land is devoted to mixed arable farming, but the light soil in these relatively frost-free areas, which extend from Chadwick Bank towards the Severn and Holt Fleet, provides ideal conditions for market gardening. Livestock tends to be limited to riverside meadows or to permanent pasture overlying the heavier Keuper Marl with its pockets of clay which make cultivation difficult even in these days of mechanised equipment. A major source of clay by the station has since 1885 provided the raw material for the present Brickworks but in earlier days the same clay was used to make the crucibles required in nearby forges. Those seeking further information on the geographical features of the County of Worcester and its effect on land utilisation are recommended to study part 68 of "The Land of Britain", a report of a land utilisation survey of Worcestershire.

It is only forty or fifty years since sixty per cent of farm work was carried out by hand: hedging and ditching; singling, hoeing, lifting and storing of root crops; cutting, stooking and thatching of the corn harvest. Even the picking up of stones - especially important in fields bordering on the Common - or the pulling of the poisonous ragwort were included in spare moments. Wages were low and one farmer today recalls how his father in the early 1900s employed ten men who worked six days a week from 6 a.m. to 6 p.m. with additional casual seasonal labour. There were six in his own family and £15.0.0 was fetched from the bank each week to pay the wages for all, with enough left over for their own housekeeping!

Every farm field was then identified and well-known by its own name which would indicate its location or its purpose for the benefit of farm workers. Many of these are still in use and provide fascinating material for further study. The names of some around the Castle are good examples, Pool Tail Meadow, Park Piece, Park Orchard, Osier Bed, Baker's Orchard, The Inning and Flax Pit Piece.

Lorry loads of perishable goods still leave the district daily for markets in Birmingham, Wolverhampton and other centres, but it is not so long ago that horse drawn waggons queued on the roads to the station to unload their cargoes into special containers for onward despatch to markets even further afield.

Combine harvesters have done away with the "Threshing

Box" which travelled from farm to farm in autumn and winter months. Several of these operated in the Hartlebury parish and their arrival was the signal for a united effort on the part of friends and neighbours and for the farmers' wives to provide generous rations of food and drink - mainly cider - to suit the special occasion. The same individual who provided the threshing equipment usually owned the facilities for making the cider, travelling with their mill and cider press to the larger orchards or operating from their home base to meet the lesser needs of the cottagers who brought their harvest to the site. Huge quantities of cider or perry, of varying quality, were produced in this way, for half a gallon or even a gallon was regarded as the normal daily ration for workers and was generally taken into account as part of wages by less than generous employers.

Modern farming methods, especially those introduced since the Second World War, have transformed the industry by making possible vastly increased production of most crops, which contrasts markedly with the long period of depression in the early part of the century. The problems associated with the need for vast capital investment for land and equipment and the apparently uncontrollable cycle of overproduction which results in "mountains" of dairy products and cereals, continue to exercise the minds of politicians, environmentalists and farmers. Thus, the closely-knit nature of the farming community in which everyone knew everybody has now been destroyed with the almost total elimination of a workforce in a highly mechanised, scientifically oriented industry. Farms of one hundred acres, which at one time provided work for ten or more men plus casual seasonal employment for women and children as well as for incomers such as gipsy families, can now operate more effectively with one or two skilled operatives.

Small units have become uneconomic if they cannot raise the capital necessary for expensive equipment and Hartlebury cannot avoid the trend for farms to become larger and the smaller units to specialise in the more intensive rearing of livestock or to increase the production of fruit and vegetables which provide a reasonable return with less capital outlay. The arrival of the "Farm Shop" and the "Pick Your Own" fruit and vegetable farms are a natural outcome of this and increasingly attractive to a more mobile urban population. Cottages once occupied by farm workers now provide homes for commuters and farm buildings, especially barns which can no longer be adapted for modern requirements, are converted into prestigious homes.

Rather than dwell any longer, however, upon what are perhaps well-known changes, a few extracts from Gaut's "History of Worcestershire - Agriculture and Rural Evolution" - which refer specifically to Hartlebury, may be of more than passing interest. Rabbits today regarded as a pest provided an additional source of income for many, especially during periods of recession, and were obviously regarded as something other than a nuisance and worthy of special note in 1757 when, "a warren on the upper end of Hartlebury Heath was stated to cover 300 acres of land on dry soil affording a good feed for coneys". "Warreners" - warren keepers - one of whom is known to have lived at Titton House, were even employed to ensure their preservation! Alive, they were sold for coursing in the Black County and dead, their pelts found their way to furriers and their carcasses to butchers.

In the late eighteenth century flax was grown in a small way and in 1782 turnips were worthy of special mention as being grown intensively for winter feed for sheep. John Griffin of Charlton sold "two pieces of turnips he called 16 acres for 21 guineas but if they turn out well 22 guineas"! Poaching and stealing of all sorts of farm produce was rife, "offenders could be imprisoned for the first offence and publicly whipped for subsequent offences" and an association "for the prosecution of felons" was formed to help deal with the problem. Whether they were hanged along with other miscreants at "Hangman's Corner" in Lincomb Lane or whipped and placed in the stocks which stood in the churchyard below the Old Grammar School is not clear! The whipping post and stocks were removed in 1839.

In the nineteenth century fortunes varied from a golden era in the middle of the century when "potatoes increased in importance" and Jerusalem artichokes were grown, "from one perch of ground, four bags fetched 15/- a bag" equivalent to £225 per acre! Hops were seldom grown, only 2 acres in 1825 and 4 acres in 1844. Further details of farming conditions in the 1840s are given in Dee Cooper's extracts from "The Journal of Emily Pepys" (p.27) In 1869 Pye Hill Farm of 41 acres was sold for £4,400, a high price in those days, but the following years heralded a long period of depression brought on by a succession of years of bad weather,

Strawberries for market

together with increasing imports from the New World, especially of cereals. In the early twentieth century "a co-operative society was started in Hartlebury to improve bargaining powers in the purchase of supplies".

In 1914 there were 22055 horses in the county, an increase associated with demands not only from farmers but from road hauliers and the war time needs of the yeomanry. Early in the First World War, however, tanks and motorised vehicles soon took the place of cavalry and horse drawn gun carriages and in the post-war period the rapid increase in the use of motor cars and farm tractors soon drove horses from the roads and fields.

Farming today is big business and a new generation trained in business and scientific methods has replaced the aristocratic land owner who controlled the destinies of rural populations for many centuries. The benefits and disadvantages of this revolution are for others to ponder over and for the future to determine.

THE GROWTH OF INDUSTRY

As with any rural parish various small pockets of cottage industries have sprung up from time to time, many of them to supply the needs of the farming community with tools or to process the results of the harvest. Doubtless, other individuals were tempted by the proximity of developing industrial centres to earn a supplement to the family income by taking on "out work" which could be done at home, but the first evidence of any major development of natural resources came with the opening of the Hartlebury Brickworks in 1885. Production has been uninterrupted since then except for the war years. During the First World War it was used for a time as a base for army horses and as a distribution centre for fodder, especially straw and hay. During the Second World War empty accommodation provided spare storage.

Many millions of red Hartlebury house bricks have emerged from the kilns over the years and it is good to know that recent alterations and extensions mean that these works, owned by the Baggeridge Brick Company since 1950 are the most modern in the country with promise of resources and skills to enable them to remain in production for many years to come. The pits which remain, being impermeable, provide suitable sites for refuse disposal and the land can thus eventually be reclaimed.

It was the prospect of a second World War, however, which brought into the district industry on a large scale and Hartlebury would probably be an even tinier speck on the map had it not been for the aggressive intentions of Adolf Hitler.

War clouds were gathering over Europe in the late 1930s when Britain's defence chiefs somewhat belatedly decided to prepare for the impending onslaught. One of their briefs was to find central storage depots - away from the potential bombing targets of the big cities yet close to the country's rail and road networks. The sites were therefore to be in a rural setting, capable of camouflage,

while being able to draw upon a skilled workforce from nearby centres of population.

The rest is history. The Royal Air Force arrived in Hartlebury and the adjoining parishes of Elmley Lovett and Rushock in 1938 to set up seven centres which were to become the 25 Maintenance Unit, providing in all a storage area of two and a quarter million square feet which has left an indelible stamp upon some 360 acres of North Worcestershire. Hundreds of new jobs were created almost overnight and for many families in the Wyre Forest towns of Kidderminster, Stourport and Bewdley - and even as far afield as the Black Country - it brought a modicum of prosperity and job security. Kidderminster's carpet barons, for so long the self-appointed arbiters of the area's labour force, had their authority challenged.

No. 25 MU had a chequered existence. The Germans never quite realised its importance during the Second World War or, if they did, never made it a target for strategic bombing. In any event, the very nature of the unit, heavily disguised, using rail links rather than roads, and scattered over vast acres, would have made its elements extremely difficult to identify and to destroy. Hartlebury thus became a vital arsenal for Britain's war effort. Components for the R.A.F. were packed by the 3,000 employees and despatched to all parts of the globe. Some new housing, mainly at Waresley, was provided to cater for the influx of key workers which brought in fresh blood and new ideas to a village which had changed little from Victorian times. Many stayed on after the war and their children and grandchildren make up much of the present generation.

The sudden development of 25 MU came as a shock to the somewhat enclosed and introverted community. At first there was resentment. Older villagers recall how they were appalled at the desecration by the Unit of the beautiful countryside with its woodland walks and fertile farmland, but with hindsight, most concede that it was a necessary intrusion. Not only was it vital for the war effort, but it provided a prosperous living for local families.

For those uprooted by the war and suddenly implanted in the heart of the Worcestershire countryside, it was just as traumatic. They experienced antagonism and it was some time before they were accepted and not treated as unwelcome "foreigners". Because they spoke with a strange accent, because they were used to a different lifestyle, they were greeted by suspicion and often hostility. Families posted to Hartlebury can recall how tradesmen were wont to refuse them goods because they were not "local". That short-sighted view has long since disappeared and there is genuine regret when the Air Ministry announced its intention in 1970 to close down the unit. The convoys of R.A.F. trucks slowly decreased. Gone were the "Queen Marys" - the giant transporters which carried the wings and fuselage of fighting planes. It was the end of an era, and the base was eventually closed in 1977, a large quanitity of surplus stores including aeroplane wings having, in the

1 Newhouse farm present home of "West Tip" 7 Elmley Lovett Church

2 Site of houses demolished by vandals 8 POW Camp WW2

3 Invading vandalising travellers camp 9 Administrative Offices of the site

4 Officers Mess now Little Bowbrook School 10 Station

5 Clay Pit 11 Station good yard

6 Brickworks

meantime, been deeply buried on the site.

For three years it lay derelict - a national asset just wasting away. Hereford and Worcester County Council, then newly formed, flirted briefly with the idea of buying the major part to revitalize the area's industry and labour market. But the £1,000,000 bid under the Community Land Act was never more than tentative and the project was not pursued.

25 M.U. Site 19

The official opening of the new Baggeridge brick plant performed by the Rt. Hon. Peter Walker, MBE, MP, Secretary of State for Energy, seen here with the Hon. P.A. Ward, the Chairman.

Right
During World War One the brick yard was used as a depot for fodder for army horses. Hay or straw was then baled by hand having been cut from the stack. Later a stationary baler was toured around and driven by a steam tractor engine

An old photograph of a steam traction engine shows how things used to be done at Hartlebury long before Baggeridge took over.

Suddenly, Hartlebury became nationally famous in a most unexpected fashion. Vandals were to succeed where Hitler had failed for an invasion took place at 25 MU. In a bid to draw attention to the shortcomings of local authorities in providing sites for itinerants, scores of caravan families homed in on the poorly protected base and soon established themselves on the sports field off Walton Lane. Some say that the families arrived at 25 MU by mistake for their target was actually Wyre Forest District Council, which was dragging its feet in coming to terms with the gipsy problem. Hartlebury, of course, is in the area of Wychavon District Council, which had already met most of its obligations by setting up two municipal gipsy sites. Nevertheless, there was to be no reasoning with the itinerants who were joined by contingents of nomads of all descriptions.

There ensued a national scandal which all lawful agencies seemed powerless to halt. Not only was the sports field ruined and the pavilion destroyed within days, but there began the systematic wrecking of rows of houses which had once been lived in by the unit's firemen, police and other emergency staff.

Because it was Ministry of Defence land, the civil police were unable to take action. The Government's Property Services Agency staff did nothing. A horrified nation saw on its television screens the effects of mob rule and unchecked vandalism. Houses were reduced to useless shells and stripped of all metal and wooden fittings. The damage bill ran to hundreds of thousands of pounds and when the caravan families were eventually cleared off by court order, the vandalised structures had to be demolished.

The village thus lost a valuable housing enclave which could have provided modestly priced homes for young couples. The unwelcome visitors moved on to the former teachers' training college at Summerfield, but prompt legal action prevented any major repetition of their vandalism.

In 1980, the threat of a further invasion was lifted when the major part of 25 MU was bought for nearly £3,000,000 by Lansdown Estates, a subsidiary of the English Property Corporation, for development as a Trading Estate. The company agreed with parish, district and county councillors that the Station Road access to the site was inadequate. It was prepared to donate £500,000 towards the improvement of Crown Lane to make it the main approach road from the A449, but a section of village opinion called for a public enquiry into the property company's plans, which included increased industrial footage within the site. The Protection Group was perfectly within its rights to do so but it caused a long hold-up until the plans which had been agreed many months before were eventually confirmed. Vital land negotiations were thus delayed so that in 1986, six years later, the roadworks had only just begun.

The present Hartlebury Trading Estate consists of the original headquarters building and Units l and 5. Having been sold to Stonehouse Investments in 1983 and again in 1986 to Peel Holdings, the emphasis has changed from "development" to "investment". Most of the original buildings covering some 1,000,000 sq. ft. have now been refurbished either by the Holding Company or tenants, at a cost of approximately £10,000,000. One hundred and twenty firms employ some fifteen hundred workers and there remains a further potential for a fifty per cent increase in building development on the site. Much of the space is used for warehousing and this includes provision for part of the E.E.C. surplus grain store.

The remaining five components of 25 MU have been similarly developed, three as other Trading Estates, one as a Royal Ordnance plc and one still retained by Government for use as yet another grain store. The officers' mess is now a part of Bowbrook School.

Another large industrial development, this time at Summerfield, also came into being as a result of the Second World War when a factory was built for the manufacture of small arms ammunition. Construction of buildings on the site commenced in 1940 and the majority of the present buildings were completed by 1942. Both the land and the buildings were Crown Property but the site was operated by Imperial Chemical Industries Limited, on behalf of H.M. Government. In 1946 the manufacturing activities ended and the site was utilised as a Ministry depot primarily for the storage of machine tools.

In 1951 under an agreement between Imperial Chemical Industries and the then Ministry of Supply, and subsequently

under arrangements between I.M.I. and the Ministry of Defence, the site was established as an Agency Factory to undertake research and development work on solid rocket motors using cast double base propellant. The establishment has been in continuous use for this purpose up to the present day and is responsible for the design, development and production of many of the rocket motors used on missiles in service with the Armed Forces. Well-known examples of these are: Rapier, Sea Dart, Swingfire and Sea Skua.

In recent times the ownership of the establishment has been ceded to Royal Ordnance plc as part of the privatisation arrangements, the site being operated by I.M.I. on their behalf.

The village is fortunate therefore to have these ready-made sources of work within the parish. It is one of the few benefits to derive from the evil of Hitler.

Workers from 25 M.U., Hartlebury, are seen arriving at the village station.

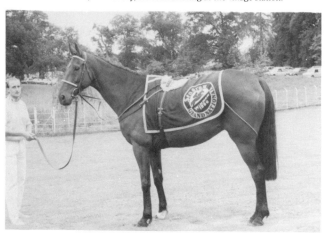

The 1986 winner of the Grand National is stabled nearby. The major scar on its hind quarters was the result of an "engagement" with a lorry leaving the Industrial Estate.

Hartlebury Gipsies. The perpetration of these acts of vandalism just described must not be ascribed to those families of gipsies who for many years lived on the Common in tents made of nut sticks and fabric and where the gipsy evangelist, Baker, held regular services in his tented chapel. A change in the byelaws in 1908 governing the use of the Common necessitated their move to two other sites, one on the Lower Heath for the Loveridges and another on Garfields Meadow in Titton for the Smiths. It was in the early 1920s that John Loveridge erected another chapel, this time timber-built and attractively furnished, which attracted visiting preachers of all denominations*.

Vandalising of Houses 1978

In the course of time most of these families were housed in Stourport. Sadly, the sites they left were gradually occupied by other itinerant groups which vandalised even the chapel. However, Hereford and Worcester County Council has now provided a permanent site at Lower Heath with modern amenities for those who prefer a less conventional way of life.

Other nomadic gipsy families from as far off as the Forest of Dean regularly returned to other parts of the parish, notably Charlton and Tugwood to set up camp in tents and caravans by the roadside and were welcomed to assist in the seasonal harvesting of vegetable and fruit crops. They were always known by the name of the farmer - Southall's gipsies at Tugwood or Moule's gipsies at Charlton - and were meticulous in sending advance notice of their impending arrival. The fondness of gipsies for unusual Christian names, frequently of biblical origin, was reflected in such examples as Shadrach, Abraham, Moses, Rebecca and Esther.

* The story is told of Oliver Baldwin, son of the Prime Minister, who gave a lift in his car to a gipsy going to fetch the maternity nurse to attend to his wife now in labour at Garfields Meadow. When asked, "What do I owe you?" he replied, "if it's a boy name him Oliver Baldwin". And so it was duly carried out and "the boy" concerned is alive today in Kidderminster.

GLEANINGS FROM THE RECENT PAST

The Parish of Hartlebury, one of the largest in the County, has seen many changes in recent years, most of which have taken place as a result of the industrial development already referred to and the bypassing of the Old Worcester Road by a dual carriageway which in effect has, by encouraging development along its route, diverted the centre of population eastwards.

Older inhabitants still refer to the seventeen hamlets which enjoyed their own identity in years gone by but, mainly for the convenience of the editor, this section will be dealt with under the headings of Village, Waresley, Crossway Green, Chadwick, Titton, Charlton, Lincomb, Summerfield and Torton. This in no way minimises the previous importance of Goldness, Leapgate, Upper and Lower Moors, the Mount, Norchard, Pansington, Pepwell, Perry House, Upper and Lower Poolands, Pyehill and Whitlenge, all of which are mentioned in earlier writings and which now serve to identify farms or residences rather than centres of population.

The Village remains the principal source of attraction, largely because of the near presence of the Castle, but this in no way, however, detracts from the relatively unspoilt character of the centre which is dominated by the Parish Church of St. James, the splendid Rectory, The White Hart Inn and the adjoining Church Endowed School. The church and school are the subject of separate contributions.

The Rectory is a well preserved example of an eighteenth century parsonage. Built in 1700 with ashlar facings and of two stories with attic dormers, it was first occupied by the Revd. James Stillingfleet, son of Bishop Edward Stillingfleet, and who became Dean of Worcester in 1726 while still continuing to hold the living at Hartlebury until 1737. Its spacious and well-maintained grounds

The Rectory

amounting to 6.3 acres included tennis or croquet lawns, a pond extending to quarter of an acre and a sizeable woodland, and provided the ideal setting for social events in the days when the living of Hartlebury was well endowed and frequently associated with other preferments, in fact a very desirable charge. Today with its twenty-seven rooms, twelve of these in the attics, it is quite unsuitable for the purpose for which it was built and now lies empty awaiting a new owner who will, it is hoped, restore it to something of its earlier dignified presence.

The White Hart & Old Bakery

The White Hart Inn, once owned by the Bishop, has changed its outward appearance little over the years. It dates from the early eighteenth century and like other inns has provided a focal point for the community - the local foxhounds regularly met here as well as at The Mitre Oak, The Mare and Colt and The Talbot. Auction sales were held here and old newspaper cuttings show advertisements for tea and for supper dances at half a crown per head (twenty-seven and a half pence)! The original stables remain, but local memories recall more vividly the horse and pony sales which followed the more famous Bromsgrove sales when dealers would trot up their purchases in the road and haggle over prices there and in the bar. The beautiful decorative hanging baskets have always been an outstanding feature of the exterior.

The only other obvious remaining evidence of more recent history indicative of the village's strategic importance lies in The Old Bakery, the sign outside belying the fact that it is now a private residence. The adjoining butcher's shop is another empty reminder of days gone by.

Quarry Bank and Inn Lane both lead up to the Old Worcester Road and both in their own way provide examples of the old and

the new in residential properties both providing a variety of attractive dwellings, many closely abutting on to the road with the old adapted to modern needs and the new blending in well on the whole with the existing houses.

Most of the new building in Quarry Bank has taken place since the Second World War as the result of the infilling of sites, previously the gardens of other properties. Myrtle Cottage is a good example, with the garden now the site of four separate properties. The narrowness of the road, cutting through sandstone outcropping has prevented further development until one reaches the higher levels at Waresley (p.61).

Visitors can be excused for not noticing The Gables, built in 1702 as an improvement to the earlier Grammar schoolhouse, or The Red House, latterly the home of the headmaster, which stand alongside the church. The lane from Quarry Bank which leads to them also leads to the later school building occupied from 1794 till 1912, and behind which stands the first Parish Room.

One of the most notable houses of this century is The Pleck built in 1912. Standing well back from the road on the right, it commands a splendid view of the surrounding countryside and is virtually unaltered. A special feature is the roof of Cumberland stone tiles, reputed to weigh some seventy-five tons.

Inn Lane, also very narrow, leaves Rectory Lane opposite the school. Here again older properties have been adapted to present-day needs and a few fine new residences built. Missing, however, is The Pepper Box, the smallest house in Worcestershire which at one time attracted much attention. Built into the north bank it measured only thirteen feet four inches by eight feet ten inches with one room up and one down. Brick built prior to 1900, it was only recently demolished.

Before joining the Old Worcester Road we find the Post Office and a Village Store which at one time included a bakery now modernised to meet increasing needs in the area. The blacksmith's shop which had developed into an agricultural engineering business has only recently closed down. The branch of the Midland Bank which opened in Hill House in 1921 was closed down during the Second World War and did not reopen.

A recent development in this area is the Regent's Gate housing estate, built on what was previously known as Waterlade. It includes The Birches, private sheltered accommodation for thirty-two elderly people in single or double flats. This provision by the Wychavon District Council is essentially for those with local connections who have lost their partners and are in need of security. There is a resident warden and limited communal facilities.

The Talbot. The oldest of the Hartlebury inns, now a "listed building", faces the top of Inn Lane on the Old Worcester Road. Recent renovation has revealed that it was a farmhouse dating from the early seventeenth century. Additions and alterations were made in the eighteenth and twentieth centuries to the original timber-framed building which stands on a sandstone plinth. Originally known as The Dog Inn because of the white pointer dog which was part only of the sign, it gave its name to that part of the old turnpike road which became known locally as Dog Lane. For a while in the early nineteenth century it was also known as The Dealers' Inn. It boasted not only a bowling green but also a quoit pitch. Quoits were iron rings, sharp-edged, weighing between seven and nine pounds, thrown from a distance of eighteen yards into a clay pit around an iron hob and scoring proceeded as in bowls. The game was popular in its day. The Talbot remained a working farm up till 1940 when it was sold and a barn converted into a skittle alley. An inventory of 1911 refers to iron spittoons in the tap room, snuff boxes in the smoke room and a selection of 950 clay pipes to go, doubtless, with the ever-popular hand-rubbed "black twist".

The original road to the Station ran behind the Inn with a butcher's shop on the opposite corner. The increased volume of traffic to the trading estate coupled with the advent of the new dual carriageway necessitated the provision of the present diversion with the loss of the shop and the closure of the old road.

The Grove House lying opposite the inn was until recently the site of a flourishing family tie factory, Vigorn Ties Ltd. founded in 1955, whose clients included many of the fashionable City outfitters. "We only sell to the higher class of tailor because they are the only people who can sell ties at our prices."

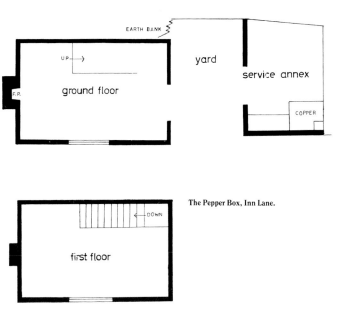

The Pepper Box, Inn Lane.

Two abortive planning applications. During 1944 and 1945 proposals were put forward on behalf of parishioners for the provision of a Parish Centre which would provide social, educational and recreational facilities. A more suitable school together with a Hall, a Club and playing fields for both parish and school were all included, the playing fields to include a full-sized football pitch, a smaller area for children, a cricket square, a bowling green and two tennis courts - all for an estimated expenditure of £8,000. Since the proposal would involve the acquisition of land in the Park owned by the Church Commissioners, their opinion was sought and a Diocesan Commission set up. Their opinion was divided between the desirability of providing such an amenity for the parish and the effect which the proposed development might have on the future of the Castle as the See House of the Diocese and the impairment of the essential character of its park. This imaginative proposal did not proceed further.

A second planning application which would have transformed the entire nature of the village was made in 1964. This involved the building of some thousand houses, spread over 118 acres of land on Moor Farm, together with shops, a school and other modern facilities. The application went to appeal, but was turned down.

Top The Talbot and Butcher's shop before road widening

Bottom Talbot Inn – today

1 Castle	6 Old Bakery
2 Church	7 Charlton
3 Rectory	8 Charlton Mill
4 Village School	9 The Gables
5 White Hart Inn	

Waresley has already been mentioned as that extension of the village approached by way of Quarry Bank which also adjoins the Old Worcester Road via Waresley Road before it in turn rejoins the new dual carriageway. It was selected as the site for residences of "the gentry" in the eighteenth and nineteenth centuries, also at one time boasting the police station and a baker's shop. Three properties are of special interest.

The Manor House dates from the early seventeenth century with additions and alterations in the late seventeenth, eighteenth and nineteenth centuries. The early part is timber-framed with wattle and daub infill and painted brick. This fascinating listed building previously known as The Manor Farmhouse has almost certainly associations with the Manor of Waresley, mentioned as belonging to William de Beauchamp, who held five hides in Waresley within Hartlebury. The history is almost certainly associated with the five "Manses" mentioned as existing in 980. It is said to have provided shelter, along with Harvington Hall, for the perpetrators of the Gunpowder Plot (1605). Depositions were taken at Hartlebury by Sir Walter Levison and James Button and Malcolm Bowyer, gentlemen who lived in Hartlebury and Kidderminster District and all well-known County Magistrates, against one Thomas Winter, one of the traitors.

From the nature of the differing floor levels, odd cupboards and a stair which runs up behind the original chimney breast, there may be substance in the tradition that priests were also sheltered here following the time of the Reformation. Land belonging to the house at one time included The Talbot Inn, part of Bishop's Wood and Waterlade, now the site of the Regent's Gate housing development. For many years in this century the house lay empty and neglected, even used as a turkey plucking house. It has now been tastefully restored by the present owners.

Waresley House was built by John Baker in the late eighteenth century. His family had been settled in Waresley for many generations and he was High Sheriff of the County in 1812. It is described by Laird as "standing between Hartlebury and Ombersley close to the high road on the eastern side. It is situated so as to command a very extensive view to the south-east and forms a large and lofty cube in a plain and neat but handsome style of architecture of modern construction; elegantly furnished, but not so as to preclude comfort: and the extent and taste of its plantations embellish the grounds and promise to do even more so when they shall arrive at their full growth. Upon the whole there is perhaps not a more comfortable residence in the County". Noake refers to the same house in 1851 as "a handsome mansion... the site of a Dame School, a Sunday School and a Dorcas Club for the supply of wearing apparel for the poor of the parish ... upwards of 4,500 garments and 3,450 yards of flannel have been provided".

For some years it was let to John Peel, brother of the then Prime Minister, Dean of Worcester Cathedral (1845-1874). His

Manor House

Waresley House

name will always be associated with the great work of restoration of that building accomplished during his term of office.

The house was bought in 1880 by the Revd. Benjamin Gibbons, Rector of Lower Mitton. He was a man of considerable means who, during his thirty-three years as Rector not only acted as a scholarly theologian but in 1881 began the building of what was later to become the Parish Church of Stourport. He was a great philanthropist, providing amongst other things a lodge in which to house his several curates. He resigned the living in Lower Mitton in 1894 after thirty-three years of devoted labour. While in Hartlebury, he and his large family lived in considerable style and the house became a centre of gracious living and generous hospitality. He travelled widely with a son who kept careful diaries, which still exist, of his various journeys, and died in 1912. Large families are usually happy ones but seem equally to be a source of many tales of escapades and pranks. The Gibbons were no different. On the occasion of the marriage of Marion, the eldest daughter, in January

1888 some members decided to mount the church tower from which to cast the rice - a custom in those days - upon the departing couple. The effect upon the horses pulling the carriage was electric, for they bolted, but no serious sequel was reported. Doubtless the culprits shared the consternation and were duly reprimanded, with the happy couple having a memorable "send off".

Members of the family continued to live in the district but best remembered are the daughters, Margaret and Frances, who built The Pleck in Quarry Lane, from the sale of a picture it is said, and who, driving around in their pony and trap, were to dominate the social scene in the village for many years. Among their many good works was the establishing and running of a VAD Convalescent Hospital at the Castle during World War One, using their own house as an annexe for the less disabled (p.30). This short account of the Gibbons period does not do justice to the wealth of material and photographic records which are available. A fuller illustrated version of this fascinating family's influence on the life of Stourport and Hartlebury would make interesting reading.

Waresley House was purchased in 1920 by Captain Allan Dyson Perrins, a member of a well-known Worcestershire family. He had a distinguished career as an officer in the Welsh Guards,

Gibbons family wedding

serving in both World Wars and for a time in 1940 a detachment of the Guards was billeted here prior to embarkation for Singapore.

It was between the wars, however, that the social activity in the house reached a new high level of hospitality and entertainment which was made possible with a staff of ten in the house, five in the gardens, plus a stud groom and two stable lads. Mrs. Perrins was a natural horsewoman who showed an unrivalled degree of elegance when mounted sidesaddle on hunters of her own

breeding and training. Many prizes were won in Hunter showing classes and she and the children followed the hunt whenever and wherever possible. The annual lawn meet in the grounds was a special occasion at a time when John Peaker, that famous huntsman, was with the Worcestershire Hunt. The Adam interior of Waresley House had a most attractive café au lait drawing room. Mrs. Perrins came to choose the exact colour during a luncheon party when she surprised the guests by removing the chocolate soufflé to show it to her decorator: "It is just the colour I want for my drawing room"! The family continued to live there until 1944.

The house was then taken over by a Catholic Order of Monks as an approved school for boys and the name changed to St. Gilbert's. In addition to the usual academic subjects, considerable emphasis was placed upon practical outdoor pursuits, including voluntary projects in the village. The spacious grounds were transformed, stable blocks and paddocks were replaced by staff houses

Benjamin Gibbons & son on safari

and the grounds altered to provide well-equipped sports facilities. In 1975 the Worcester County Council acquired the building, again for teenage boys in need of care and supervision. With the increasing tendency to keep youngsters in their own community, the number of pupils has fallen and its future is currently being reviewed. *

Mrs. Allan Dyson Perrins

Meet of Worcestershire fox hounds at Waresley House

* St. Gilbert's. The Social Services Department of Hereford and Worcester County Council have recently indicated that they will no longer use the facilities at St. Gilbert's after July 1987. Once this decision becomes effective, various options will be available and other Departments, including the Local Education Authority, will be expected to declare their interest. A residential and day establishment for children deemed to be maladjusted or behaviourally difficult is one possibility. Since February 1986 one unit - the Dormy Unit - has been used temporarily as a day unit for such children pending the search for more appropriate buildings in the Bromsgrove-Redditch area.

Waresley Court was the third important residence in Waresley. No date of its origin can be traced but its heyday certainly appears to have been in the late nineteenth or early twentieth century when it was first the home of Mr. John Watson and later Lord Hampton. Letters from Mr. Watson's daughter in the Parish Magazine in 1899 give a clear picture of that period which is confirmed by a later contribution from a son.

Their father spent his leisure time breeding race horses and built up a nationally famous stud. One of his horses won the Oaks and many others of his yearlings fetched record prices at Doncaster Sales. The sight of a string of young horses passing down to the station for transportation is recounted to this day. These had previously been exercised on meadows by the railway line, presumably to accustom them to the prospect of their journey. His son writes, "Even we in a quiet way had seven servants indoors and nine out, not counting farm hands", and adds, "My father was an old gentleman of old fashioned habits, a keen hunting man but the staff all liked him in spite of his rages". His daughter also writes, "Sunday afternoon was a wearisome time - father thought we ought not to leave the grounds. I suppose he thought it was not respectable because all the men and maids were out then in various stages of courting and walking out!"

The stud itself included four separate yards, one for hunters and carriage horses, one for yearlings, one covered and a fourth "the lower boxes". It was complete with blacksmith's shop, carpenter's bench, a gasometer for lighting the stables plus the necesary barns with their chaff cutters and oat grinders.

On his death, the stud was dispersed, the property sold to the Revd. Benjamin Gibbons and in 1897 it became the home of Lord and Lady Hampton. They died in 1905 and 1907 respectively to be succeeded by a son who stayed on at the Court with his sister, the Hon. Mary Pakington. Both remained unmarried, were much respected and are well remembered today. He was an officer in the Worcestershire Yeomanry, a friend of Baden Powell and became much involved in the Scout movement. His own troop, based on the Court, enjoyed splendid facilities and the story is told of how they were in camp at Talybont in 1914 when war broke out. They struck camp, returned to Hartlebury, and each Scout received 1/1d. as the unexpended balance of the five shillings which they had paid in advance for the week's camp! The Hon. Mary Pakington was also very active in the Parish and, among other things, helped her brother with the "Cubs" and established a successful Choral Society.

The Court was sold in 1926 to a builder who proceeded to demolish it and then, over a period of some years, to transform the site into the present housing estate. The houses fronting on to Waresley Road came first, and much of the material for their construction came from the Court, rough cast being used to cover over the diversity of bricks used. Three blocks of flats, faced with

Lord Hampton, Hon. Mary Pakington with scout troop

The Lion, or The Crown as it was originally known - the Lion referred to the figure over the Crown on the pub sign - was a great loss but, situated as it was directly abutting upon the A449, it constituted a considerable hazard with the faster moving modern traffic. Visitors came from far and near in the early part of this century to enjoy the home brewed beer, "brewed without an ounce of sugar" and the famous rook or pigeon pie. The proprietor of that era, Mr. J. Biddle, played a dual role, acting as coachman to Captain Perrins of Waresley House and provider of a horse-drawn taxi service, "Biddle's Fly" used for short journeys, or a "Brake" for larger parties. The bowling green with its walnut tree was renowned for its peculiar bias, favouring as it did those with local knowledge! The "wishing well" which provided the water for the hostelry was filled in at the time of the road widening but arrangements are being made for the superstructure to be re-erected when the new roundabout planned for this site is completed. The lodge and the inn both gave way to the road alterations of 1936.

Crown Lane junction before road widening

Cornish stone, were built after the War by the District Council to house families employed at the R.A.F. Maintenance and I.C.I. Units and to provide for local needs. Other houses followed in due course to complete this development, Waresley Green as we know it today, which surrounds an area designated for recreation, with its fine tennis courts.

The Village Hall in the same area is a good example of a successful community effort. Opened in 1955, it was built to commemorate the Coronation of Queen Elizabeth. Local fund-raising enabled work to start in 1954 and to be completed within fifteen months, largely the result of voluntary effort. Boys from St. Gilbert's School dug out the foundations and local craftsmen gave freely of their time and expertise so that the final cost was kept down to £4522 and the building was free from debt within three years. It provides excellent facilities for the many local organisations as well as those outside agencies which choose to use them.

Another hall in the same area built after the Second World War belongs to the British Legion and provides an additional social centre much appreciated by its members.

Crown Lane a short distance to the South from Waresley crosses the dual carriageway and displays no evidence of its earlier importance. It was the site of The Lion Inn with the main entrance to Waresley House nearby. This latter building had an interesting history in that it was a replacement built in the early part of this century for the original lodge, totally destroyed during a violent storm which removed the roof and brought down a large tree on top of the remains.

Crossway Green lies further south still on the A449. Situated on the boundary of the parish with Ombersley, it was the natural reception area for the greeting of distinguished visitors en route from Worcester to Hartlebury Castle. Today its main claim to recognition lies in the venerable mitre oak and the hostelry of the same name. It is here that the A4025 from Stourport joins the main road and for many years the site was known as "Bissett's Corner".

Mr. and Mrs. Bissett had recently retired after World War One to enjoy their small holding of ten acres. A motor bicycle was a recent acquisition. One day a motorist called to say that his Model T Ford car had run out of petrol; could they help for there was no source nearer than Kidderminster or Worcester. A passing remark from the driver after having been supplied with the necessary fuel, "Why don't you start selling petrol here? It's an ideal place", prompted Mrs. Bissett, always the business brains of the family, to contact Shell Oil Company and so the petrol station began with a few five gallon drums and a sign, "Fill up here with Shell". With a halfpenny charge on each gallon throughput in lieu of rent, a pump was later installed and eventually all the main proprietary brands were available. The station never sought to develop as a service garage but did later provide for simple repairs and a small shop for cigarettes and confectionery as well as bed and breakfast facilities. It is easy to understand how the area became known as "Bissett's Corner".

The Congregational Chapel already referred to (p. 43) stood on the opposing corner of the road and both it and the garage also gave way to the present dual carriageway.

St. Mary's Church, once regularly supported, is now used only as a cemetery chapel. Local inhabitants, along with those of Chadwick, Titton and Lincomb, still recall with a degree of nostalgia the days when church services were regularly held here, the only common meeting ground, apart from the Titton Inn, where acquaintances could meet and friendships be sustained.

The Mitre Oak is only one of several claimants in the district to the title of the "Apostles Oak", others being at Great Witley and Martin Hussingtree. Tradition has it that St. Augustine, the Apostle of the English, met the British Bishops in 603. Campden in his report states that, "After some squabbling about the observance of Easter, the preaching of the Gospel and the sacrament of baptism administered according to the Romish Church, they separated with little agreement". It may well be that it was simply a boundary mark of the Manor on the route from Worcester and a meeting place for Gospel readings. Trees were commonly used in early days to mark the boundaries in forested areas. Whatever the truth is, the tree itself with the mitre-shaped defect on its trunk, still provides a well-known landmark in the County and has given its name to a succession of local hostelries on the site. It is now in an advanced state of decay and just to confound future historians still further, another oak was planted by Bishop Philpott in 1887 on the opposite side of the A449 within the grounds of the inn. This was said to be a scion of the original but considerable doubt is now being cast on the veracity of this claim.

The Mitre Oak Inn of today is a modern residential hotel built in 1936 to replace the centuries-old hostelry and coaching inn burned down in 1930. This original building faced towards Worcester city with the old single track Bristol to Holyhead road behind. The old coach house and stables were later converted into garages. The half-timbered hostelry became known as "The Friendly Inn" being used for local meetings of the Oddfellows and other Friendly Societies. The present building bears no resemblance to its predecessor but does bear witness to it in the form of a large

Forester's Fete

Bissett's Corner

Bissett's Garage

fireplace in the restaurant representing a replica of the Mitre Oak tree outside fashioned in oak with intricate carved details of local wildlife.

Club Walks and Fairs were a feature of many rural parishes in the late nineteenth and early twentieth centuries. Club Walks were organised by the Friendly Societies, precursors of the national

The Mitre Oak

Mitre Oak site today

St. Mary's Chapel

Central Electricity Generating Board power station

sickness and social security schemes and were normally associated with processions to church headed by the local band and traditionally dressed, in the case of Hartlebury, as Robin Hood and his Merry Men. A Maypole was commonly erected on the village green with sports or other entertainment to provide a family day out around Easter or Whitsun.

Other Fairs were held with the main purpose of hiring farm and other labour, each candidate displaying an index of his occupation: a tuft of cow hair for a cowman, whipcord for a carter, wool for a shepherd or a mop for a maidservant. Colourful occasions no doubt, but embarrassing for those with lesser talents to offer.

To the east lie Norchard and Pepwell, almost certainly "berewicks" or hamlets within the Manor of Waresley, with seventeenth and eighteenth century farm houses at Stoney Lane and Yew Tree. Nearby Tugwood was a site favoured by the "Tugwood Gipsies", regular seasonal visitors for many years.

Bishop's Wood which lies behind the inn is but a shadow of its former self. From some two hundred acres in the nineteenth century, this ancient woodland is now reduced to forty-one, the remainder having been cleared for agricultural purposes to the dismay of conservationists. What is left now belongs to the Central Electricity Generating Board, and is the site for a modern plant built in 1970 to provide for an ever increasing demand for an efficient and economical supply of electricity for nearby urban and industrial communities. The site was chosen after much deliberation and the plant, which occupies only six acres, is situated in a bowl in the middle of the wood and in accordance with statutory requirements laid down to safeguard the local environment, is screened by natural and man-made landscaping.

In 1972 the Board offered to the Worcestershire Education Authority the opportunity for use by schools of the mixed woodland surrounding the sub-station and provided a classroom building to act as a base. The Local Education Authority, in turn, agreed to the provision of furnishing and material necessary for field work and for the study of Natural History of the Woodland. Voluntary Wardens are provided, a teachers' handbook is available which includes details of a nature trail and a key to the wildlife which may be encountered.

The woodland is maintained by the Board and its presence does compensate to some extent for the loss of the original much larger natural history resource. So far the facilities have been used mainly by organised school parties, a practice which is increasing, but specialist adult groups are also encouraged and individual research workers also use the site (45 different species of fungi were recently recorded by one individual).

Chadwick, now the horticultural centre of the parish, with its farm shops and Pick Your Own fruit and vegetable enterprises, is on the turnpike road from Crossway Green to Stourport, the A4025. Spe-

cial interest lies in Parsons Lane which runs from here to the village. Its name is a reminder not only of its association with Glebe Farm and Argate Cellar, but that it was along this route that the bulk of the stone was hauled for the rebuilding of the parish church, one hundred and fifty years ago. The quarry from which it originated, now overgrown, lies only a few yards from the junction with the A4025. A Black Pear tree, one of the few remaining in the County, stands nearby, another reminder of earlier days, for its sable-coloured fruit is emblazoned on the coat of arms of the County of Worcester. Argate Cellar: situated within the glebe land it is said to have been a hermit's cave and later used by various eccentrics. It is cut into the rock in a secluded part of a meadow, some eighteen feet by twelve feet and seven feet high. Its roof is supported by two pillars and two deeply splayed holes are cut in the wall, possibly sleeping bunks.

Titton was always an important hamlet, standing astride the lower end of the Titton Brook. Pansington Farm House occupies a commanding position overlooking the Lower Heath and the present building is of late seventeenth century construction with extensions and alterations in the eighteenth and twentieth centuries. Tradition places a building on this site in a much earlier period as a strategically situated outpost of the Castle, capable of commanding a view of the activity around the Redstone Ford. Built of brick with timber frame and brick infill, the outbuildings include a four bay barn, also timber-framed but weatherboarded, standing on a sandstone ashlar plinth. The tall adjacent granary, now derelict, has a communicating passage leading to the house. The extensive view of the area from this elevated situation, at one time virtually uninterrupted down to the river, now includes a large industrial development, a busy marina and caravan park, all occupying that part of the Lower Heath taken over by Stourport Urban District in 1933.

Titton has, however, retained much of its rural interest with many delightful paths to tempt the rambler. That starting from the main road opposite Pansington and leading to Lincomb begins with the ABC steps, once twenty-six, now twenty-three in number. They have recently been restored and are subject to a preservation order. The path passes Titton Hill Farm and leads on to the escarpment overlooking the Severn Valley, this part of the journey affording the rambler extensive views of the surrounding countryside before reaching the river at Lincomb Weir. The Tannery or Tan House is situated below the ridge by the main entrance to a caravan site. Built in 1702, it now lies vacant, a sad reminder of its earlier importance. Clareland, the one time home of Eliot Howard, overlooks the same area. Its elevated situation and proximity to the river must have provided an ideal centre from which to conduct his researches.

Titton Lane provides the main access to the Tan House and

Caravan Park already mentioned, but for the more curious it also leads to "The Barracks", a small but forbidding building set off to the right. Tradition has it that this had associations with the Civil War when Hartlebury Castle was under siege. Much more likely is that it was used during the Napoleonic Wars and later became the headquarters of the Stourport Rifle Corps, a volunteer force set up in 1859 at a time when France, under Napoleon III, was again pursuing an aggressive foreign policy. Manoeuvres, exercises and camps certainly took place on the Common for some years and a Rifle Range was set up with butts on the steep face of the western slope of the hill. Long-range firing points required shots to pass over the main Stourport-Worcester road, warning flags being posted when in use.

Pansington

Titton Inn is inconspicuously situated on rising ground overlooking the A4025. Originally an ale or cider house in a cottage of two rooms and a kitchen, it has gradually been extended and upgraded. The bowling green is now overgrown but a skittle alley has been added for the entertainment of those who enjoy a game with their drink. Recent alterations to the alley revealed that the joists came from jigs used in the assembly of Vampire fighter planes and that much of the rest of the structure consists of those robust boxes used for the packing and transportation of rifles during World War Two. Presumably these were obtained following the cessation of wartime operations and dismantling of the nearby R.A.F. Maintenance Unit. On the wall in the Lounge hangs a picture showing "The Rules of this Lodging House" at a time when it was an old Cornish Inn owned by West Country Brewers. It gives no date, but some of the long list of instructions are worth quoting:

"Fourpence a night for bed"
"Sixpence for supper"
"No more than three in a bed"
"No boots to be worn in bed"
"No razor grinders taken in"
"Organ grinders to sleep in the attick"

The landlord of the day was one Isakah O'Donovan.

Tan House

Hillditch Lane leads past Titton Mill en route to Charlton. The motive power of water has been a source of energy for many centuries and water-powered millwheels were commonly set up to drive machinery for corn grinding, the fulling of cloth to render it more dense and therefore more waterproof, or for forging, the latter more commonly used to provide tools or equipment for the farmers, but easily converted to the fabrication of primitive weapons of war in time of need. The Titton Brook with its pools at Charlton and Hillditch provided ideal supplies of water and the mills at Charlton and Titton are known to have been used for corn grinding up to the first part of this century. The Titton Mill was of the overshot variety with buckets made of iron; that at Charlton of the more conventional type of wooden construction. The present mill at Titton was erected in 1815/17 as is evidenced by a key stone over the doorway.

Titton Mill

Other mills at Lincomb and on the Stour were put out of action following the construction of the weir at Lincomb which raised the water level by four to six feet.

The lane follows the stream and on to the pool of the same name but leaves it here on its way to Charlton. For those who prefer to walk, the pathway through the Hillditch Coppice follows the stream and offers a veritable profusion of wildlife for the naturalist, as well as providing a reminder that the raw material for washing baskets, trugs and other carriers, so essential to the country family, came from the osier beds here. Most of these beds throughout the country are now neglected but there was a time when the special variety of willow, its saplings made pliable by steaming, was carefully cultivated and harvested just as any other crop. The road rejoins the stream and the path before joining the B4193 at Charlton.

Charlton One of the more important of the original hamlets lies only a short distance from the village on the Stourport road and gives its name to the pool which lies to the west of the Castle and which added to the defences of that building. Those elegant nineteenth century residences, Charlton House and Charlton Farm House occupy a commanding position overshadowing the White Cottage which was built to provide a residence for Chaplains to the Bishop. The ale house which stood on the south corner of Charlton Lane, with its sign, "Ale, Porter and Cider" painted on the wall has only recently been demolished.

The main contribution, however, to the parish lay in those activities centred on the mill with its associated forge, carpenter's and wheelwright's shops which all derived their power from the water which fed from the pool. Here corn was ground until the early part of this century, agricultural implements and other implements were forged and the carpenter plied his trade. One of its most respected owners of the present century added building to the enterprise - he built the present school - but such was his generosity to others and his demand for the highest standards of workmanship that he remained a comparatively poor man. One employer is known to have added a bonus to an account in recognition of this, realising the slender nature of any profit margin likely to accrue. The forge which lay on the opposite side of the Stourport road had its own mill race but ceased to function in the 1920s when the level of the pool was reduced. Evidence of its previous existence remains in the ruins of a brick building. A cider mill was also operated here - one of several in the parish - to provide that essential ingredient for the quality of life in the rural communities of those days. A flood following a storm in 1881 seriously damaged the mill.

Opposite the mill in Hillditch Lane was the pound, an enclosure dug out from the sandstone to provide a haven for stray animals, and a saw mill with its saw pit and later power driven machinery which provided the raw material for the carpenter. The

fact that these huge tree trunks which lay by the roadside would one day provide timber for coffins was a macabre reminder not unrecognised by parishioners! The site is now occupied by a building contractor.

View over Lower Heath

The "Barracks"

The story of the catastrophic flood at Charlton is graphically told thus:

On the sixteenth day of August in the year of our Lord one thousand eight hundred and seventy nine the Parish of Hartlebury and Neighbourhood was visited by a very severe thunderstorm accompanied by a most unusually heavy downpour of rain which continued with such violence and for such a length of time as to cause serious damage, flooding many places causing landslips of more or less importance, in others washing away the Roads etc.. and turning what are usually rippling streams into turbulant torrents, the rapid accumulation of water in the Pools and Reservoirs carried away the dams in nearly all cases but more notably the Embankment forming the dam to the Mill Pool situated within the ground to the Castle of Hartlebury, the Buildings at Charlton Mill suffering considerable damage by the Catastrophe, the Public Road leading through Hartlebury to Stourport passing over this Embankment was destroyed and vehicular traffic could only be carried on by making a considerable detour, this being a Public highway but the Pool and Mill being private property the question of liability to repair was raised by some of the Parishioners and in all probability would not have been easily settled, had not the Right Revd. Henry Phillpot D.D. Bishop of Worcester who resided at the Castle have cut the Gordian Knot by undertaking the responsibility of relieving the ratepayers and ordering the works to be done, this Plan sheweth an appearance of the place the day after the Flood, the details of the works as restored and a General view after Restoration.

The Mill House is now converted into an attractive dwelling. One of the mill wheels stands free in the forecourt and the stream which previously provided the motive power becomes a feature of the garden before continuing through Hillditch Coppice. One of the special features of the old Mill House was the two-seater privy placed over the stream, an excellent hygienic arrangement with no disposal problems.

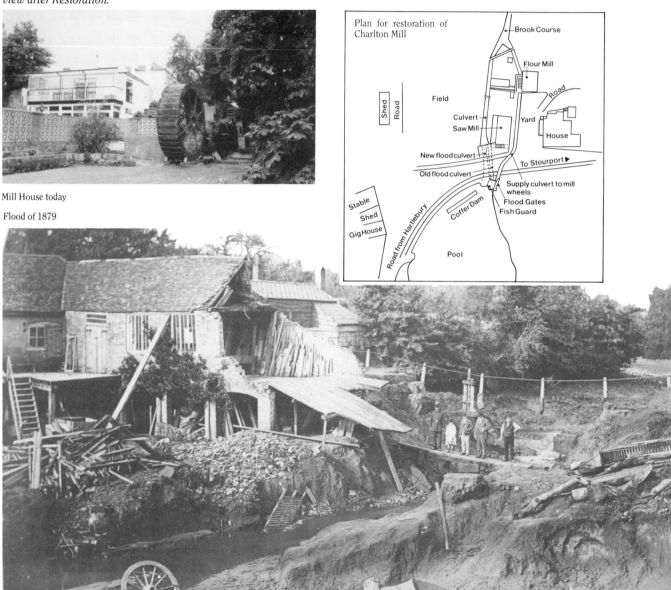

Mill House today

Flood of 1879

Plan for restoration of Charlton Mill

Brook Course

Flour Mill

Road

Field

Shed

Road

Culvert

Saw Mill

Yard

House

New flood culvert

To Stourport ▶

Old flood culvert

Supply culvert to mill wheels

Road from Hartlebury

Coffer Dam

Flood Gates

Fish Guard

Stable

Shed

Gig House

Pool

Lincomb and Summerfield are the two areas of the parish not included so far in this chapter but for very different reasons. Summerfield at the northern extremity with its small church and its own village hall naturally regarded itself as a "village" on its own, but its recent history has been overshadowed not only by the loss of these two important community centres but by the industrial development which now dominates it and which inevitably links it with nearby Kidderminster. Lincomb, on the other hand, lies to the extreme south, isolated between the Severn and the A4025 in an area designated as green belt and spared from "development". It has thus retained its rural identity and is also proud of its independence.

Summerfield for many years enjoyed a communal existence which centred on St. John's Chapel, a Memorial Hall, the Mare and Colt Inn and a general store and Post Office. The Memorial Hall, erected by public subscription to commemorate the dead of the First World War, proved to be a popular meeting place for the many and various local organisations as well as providing facilities for dances, whist drives, flower shows, etc. at a time when other entertainments in Hartlebury village or nearby Kidderminster could only be reached on foot, by bicycle or, for the privileged few, by car.

The arrival of the I.C.I factory in 1940 brought in many workers, but from considerable distances, who contributed little to the welfare of the village using only the club and canteen facilities provided by the factory and disappearing after their shift was completed, some to hostels at Shenstone, the majority to homes further afield. Those few who elected to live locally, previously mostly urban dwellers, naturally preferred to use the facilities in Kidderminster for their entertainment and recreation.

Perhaps it was a demand for more sophisticated pleasures which was to encourage the idea that the Village Hall, which had served the community so well for nearly thirty years, should be replaced after the Second World War by something more ambitious in the shape of a Men's Club. Built on the same site with additional accommodation for a car park, it provided licensed premises with facilities for darts, billiards and snooker, as well as a lounge and hall capable of accommodating up to two hundred and fifty persons for such activities as Bingo. Membership grew rapidly to a peak of a thousand drawn from far afield. Many well-known personalities became members and the standard of snooker, billiards and darts was sufficient to support many teams in local leagues as well as attracting outstanding guest players to give exhibitions of their skill. It is understandable that many local villagers who remembered the Memorial Hall with affection were less attracted to the new Club. This more ambitious venture was not to survive the economic pressures of the 1970s and was eventually closed in 1978. It has recently been purchased and developed into a block of flats.

With the declining influence of the church, now only used for occasional services, the village is thus deprived of any focal

point upon which to fasten and maintain its social activities. Only the Mare and Colt and the general store and post office remain to serve the needs of the local populace, for the I.M.I factory which has replaced the I.C.I. unit also largely attracts its labour force from far afield and continues to provide its own club facilities for employees.

The Mare and Colt is relatively modern, built in the early nineteenth century as a village inn and called "The Cross Cloth House". The origin of the present name is not known. It has recently been considerably enlarged, although the original outline can still be identified.

Mare and Colt Inn and Post Office, Summerfield

St. John's Chapel

Shenstone, although outside the parish boundary, has a history which is closely related to the industrial development in Hartlebury brought about by the Second World War, and its story is of sufficient interest to be worthy of space here. Hostel accommodation was urgently required to house civilian workers "conscripted" to the war effort who were displaced from their own homes and a forty-four acre site at Shenstone was selected to house some thousand workers in hutted buildings.

Immediately after the War, half of the site was acquired by the Ministry of Education and converted into a Training College, with accommodation for six hundred students, to help meet the urgent demand for teachers, many of the existing staff who had kept the schools going during the emergency being only too anxious to retire.

"Shenstone" College moved to Bromsgrove in 1963 but the site was immediately re-opened to accommodate another teacher training college devoted solely to women and under the name of "Summerfield". It continued to operate until 1976/77 when the two colleges merged on the site at Bromsgrove.

Meanwhile the other half which had been retained to provide housing for displaced persons from Eastern Europe especially Poland and later, Anglo Egyptians displaced following the Suez Crisis of 1956, was sold to a consortium which now leases the buildings for intensive poultry rearing.

The buildings used by the College lay empty for many years and a restriction placed upon their use "for educational purposes only" greatly hampered any possible development, a Holiday Home and a Leisure Centre having been suggested. The vacuum thus created encouraged those itinerant travellers who had squatted and vandalised 25 MU in 1978 to move in, with further damage perpetrated here before they could be moved on.

It was not until 1985 that a suitable purchaser came forward in the form of an Islamic Charity - Madina Tul Ulcum al Islamiya. The twenty-two acre site will now be developed as an Islamic College for Girls "to promote the advancement of education and the Islamic faith". Four hundred students will be accommodated in nine H blocks with a percentage of places reserved for overseas applicants. The full course of study will last for some six years and the first entry is expected in 1986.

Lincomb, as already indicated, has retained its rural identity. Farming remains the primary industry although much of the land, following the national trend, is now controlled by fewer owners. The large pocket of market gardening which lies between Chadwick Bank and Holt Fleet extends into the area but not to the exclusion of arable crops and large specialised intensive poultry units.

Grove Farm House is "listed" as having been built in the early seventeenth century, "raised" in the late seventeenth century with later nineteenth and twentieth century alterations. Standing as it does isolated and well maintained, it presents a fine example of a timber-framed building with painted brick infill standing on a sandstone plinth. Lincombe Hall at one time the home of the Lingen family, one of whom was Secretary to the Treasury in 1870 and made Lord Lingen in 1885, was largely rebuilt in 1874 but part of an original seventeenth century house remains. At one time it

Grove Farm House

Lincomb Lock

Lincomb Weir

Lincomb Hall

was suggested that it be purchased and the house and grounds developed as a remedial home for delinquent children, but with local opposition the project was not pursued.

Proposals were made as early as 1784 for the improvement of the River Severn with the object of bringing the sea ports as far inland as possible. The project was opposed by riparian landowners and abandoned until 1835 when a proposal to create a draught of twelve feet by dredging between Gloucester and Worcester was opposed by Gloucester, but the construction of a succession of weirs to provide a draught of six feet as far up as Lincomb was eventually agreed. A trial weir at Lincomb three hundred feet long with a drop of seven feet at low water was opened in 1843 and, having withstood the current, floods and frosts of the winter, was completed in 1844 when a barge passed through the lock, one hundred feet long and twenty feet wide, in three minutes. The alteration of water level resulted in legal action by a miller on the Stour on account of rendering his mill useless. He was awarded £500 damages but a new trial was ordered and the case did not proceed, presumably because of the costs of further litigation. The same raising of the water level above the Weir resulted in the submerging of the ford at Redstone. This lock is the busiest on the

Severn and is used by over 9000 craft in the year with peaks, still rising, of 150 per day in the high season.

It is worth remembering that when the Severn was the main arterial waterway from Bristol to the Midlands, "trows" were a common sight and that any "shallows", where fording was possible, presented considerable problems. Cargoes might have to be disembarked and transferred to other craft if boats could not be manhandled through the obstacle. This accounted for the siting along the river of many wharfs and ale houses - very necessary for the rest and refreshment of the men who were either waiting for work or exhausted after their labours.

Yew Tree Cottage – Torton

Torton today displays little evidence of its earlier importance. Isolated to some extent from the other hamlets in the area it established its own local industries in Torton Lane. It is here that we find Yew Tree Cottage, possibly one of the oldest buildings in the parish. Listed as early seventeenth century, the presence of three cruck trusses in the older section would seem to indicate an earlier period. This was the site for the operations of the blacksmith and wheelwright, while the adjacent saw mill provided the raw material for this and the carpenter's enterprise on the opposite side of the lane at Carpenter's Cottage. Torton Farmhouse, also in the lane, is early eighteenth century and evidence of a stone corn mill remains here. Perry House (1741) is the oldest of several prestigious houses in the area, the others being Goldness, Glenwood and Parkmore all being of nineteenth century origin. A more recent planning application for a Motel in the area was not approved. Records of Torton Estate along with those of Lincomb, Norchard, Pooland, Titton and Waresley, as well as those held by the Bishopric, lie in the County Record Office awaiting their research, but it would appear that all were largely broken up shortly after the First World War, during that period of depression when many of the landed gentry were forced to retrench.

The Severn at Ironbridge "The Kings Highway"
(Courtesy Ironbridge Gorge Museum Trust)

The selection of illustrations from the many available is always difficult. Space permits of the reproduction of a few more which may be of more than passing interest.

1. **Titton House** – one time home of the Coney Warrener.

2. Welcome to Bishop Yeatman-Biggs 1905.

3. **Whitlenge House** – Early 19th century. The home provided by the Bishop for his secretary.

4. **Brook Cottage** – Titton
   The birth place of Hannah Best, mother of Sir William Gosse 1849-1928 – Librarian at British Museum and later, 1904-19, in the House of Lords. An authority on French and Scandinavian literature. His childhood was shadowed by the narrow tenets of the Plymouth Brethren.

5. Cider apple mill at Pepwell.

1

2

3

4

5

6

9

Hartlebury Village.

7

10

8

6. **Perry House** – Torton
Listed as "probably 1741", date stone in east wall, reset in blocked window. Early C19 with late C20 alterations.

7. Early picture of the Village showing Lodge to the Castle and Church still with its pinnacles.

8. **Clareland** Home of H-Eliot Howard for 40 years.

9. **The Pleck.**

10. **Mr. James Pugh** of Crossway Green, a licensed dealer in tea and coffee pictured with his wife outside their shop in 1890.

EPILOGUE

It was Robert Louis Stevenson who said that a preface "is more than an author can resist for it is the reward of his labours". An epilogue on the other hand provides the writer with an opportunity to apologise for any errors of omission or commission and I take the occasion to do just that, for unfortunately time and space available have not permitted a more detailed research or the inclusion of much interesting material nor the reproduction of much otherwise suitable illustrative material.

And so we come to the conclusion of a fascinating glimpse into the history of Hartlebury with the realisation that much more could have been included. On the other hand it is often wise to stop when the appetite has been whetted and to leave the reader to pursue his or her own special interest on the basis of what I hope is an acceptable introduction.

As with all parishes the past is inextricably bound up with the presence of the church and in this Hartlebury is exceptionally indebted to the presence of the home of a Bishop of Worcester for many centuries. The new era which began somewhat dramatically in 1956 is now firmly established to the envy of many other Sees, and in common with all rural parishes, we find many other changes in this century which have inevitably followed upon the transformation taking place in the society in which we live.

In addition, however, to any sense of inadequacy one may have, many simple things will remain indelibly imprinted in one's memory. In particular, I cherish the many discoveries I have made in this survey of a parish through which I have so blindly travelled for many years; the friendly people, the attractive countryside, the sympathetically restored seventeenth and eighteenth century houses and the many new dwellings built to provide accommodation for an ever-increasing new population. Perhaps I may be forgiven, however, for giving pride of place to that fascinating address Bumble Hole, Bramble Lane, Bugle Gate, set in a unspoilt corner of the parish, and in so doing, express the hope that it may long retain not only its unique title but also the charm of its isolation.

The Bumble Hole Bramble Hollow Bugle Gate dated 1620 formerly three cottages – recently sympathetically restored and converted to one house. At one time the site of a Toll Gate to control traffic to the Hampstall crossing of the Severn. The house and an adjoining 17th Century barn which was removed from Clay Green Farm Alfrick, restored and re-erected on this site c1979, a good example of timber framed buildings on sandstone plinth with veneered infill panels.

BIBLIOGRAPHY

	Victoria History of the Counties of England. Worcestershire. 4 volumes and index.		1901, 1906, 1913, 1924, 1926
Allies, J.	Antiquities & Folklore of Worcestershire.	John Russell Smith	1852
Buchanan, K.M.	The Land of Britain, Worcestershire.	Geographical Publications	1944
Cooke, G.A.	A Topographical and Statistical Description of the County of Worcester.	Sherwood, Neely & Jones	N.D.
Dyer, C.	Lords and Peasants in a Changing Society. The Estates of the Bishopric of Worcester 680-1540.	Cambridge University Press	1980
Fraser, M.	Companion into Worcestershire.	Methuen & Co.	1947
Gaut, R.C.	History of Worcestershire Agriculture and Rural Evolution.	Worcestershire Press	1939
Girouard, M.	Life in the English Country House: a social and architectural history.	York University Press	1978
Guttery, D.R.	The Great Civil War in Midland Parishes.	Cornish Bros.	1951
Habington, T.	Survey of Worcestershire. 4 vols.	Worcs. Hist. Soc.	1895-99
Haines, R.M.	The Administration of the Diocese of Worcester in the first half of the Fourteenth Century.	S.P.C.K.	1965
Iredale, D.	Discovering Local History	Shire Publications	1973
Laird, F.C.	A Topographical and Historical Description of the County of Worcester.	Sherwood, Neely & Jones	1820
Mawer & Stenton	Place Names in Worcestershire.	Cambridge University Press	1927
Miller, G.	The Parishes of the Diocese of Worcester. Vol. 2.	Hall & English	1890
Nash, T.R.	A History of Worcestershire. 2 vols.		1781-82
Pearce, E.H.	Hartlebury Castle.	S.P.C.K.	1926
Pepys, E.	Journal of Emily Pepys.	Prospect Books	1984
Pevsner, N.	The Buildings of England, Worcestershire.	Penguin	1968
Robertson, D.	The History of the Parish of Hartlebury.	Worcs. Dioc. and Arch. Soc.	1902
Tucker, Zaluckyj & Alma	Hartlebury Common - a Social and Natural History.	Hereford & Worcester County Council	1986
Turberville, T.C.	Worcestershire in the 19th Century.	Longman Brown	1852
Watson, Kenrick	Statistical and General History of Worcestershire: Parish of Hartlebury.	Worcs. Nat. Hist. Soc.	1839
Wedley, I.L.	Stourport, Rise & Decline & Final Triumph.	Kidderminster Shuttle	1933/35
Willis - Bund	Legendary History of Worcestershire.	Worcs. Arch. & Arch. Soc. Vol. XXI	1912
Willis - Bund	Social Life in Worcestershire in first quarter of C17.	Worcs. Arch. Soc. Vol. XXIII	1896
Woods, Robin	An Autobiography.	S.P.C.K.	1986
	Bishops' Registers.	Worcestershire Historical Society	